NEXT STOP GRAND CENTRAL

A TRIP THROUGH TIME ON NEW YORK'S METROPOLITAN AREA COMMUTER RAILROADS

by
STAN FISCHLER

Research Editors

Morgan Hughes
Miranda Martinez
Vincent Losinno

THE BOSTON MILLS PRESS

A water-stop completed Long Island engine #24 prepares to depart.
– courtesy John Krause

This book is being dedicated to a pair of couples who have been near and dear to me. They are Jack and Anne Goldstein of Marlboro, New Jersey, who have been friends in the truest sense of the word.

The other couple, Howard and Suzanne Samelson of New York City, inspired this book with their marvelous Broadway Limited antique store and their constant help on my various railroad projects.

Last but certainly not least, my eternal thanks to Shirley Fischler, devoted wife, researcher, typist, grammarian and helper in the clutch when the project seemed to be derailed. Without Shirley, no book.

Fischler, Stan, 1932-
    Next stop Grand Central

ISBN 0-919783-22-8

1. Railroads – Northeastern States – History.
2. Railroads – Northeastern States – Commuting traffic – History.   I. Title.

TF23.1.F57   1986   385'.0974   C86-093446-2

Stan Fischler, 1986

Published by:
THE BOSTON MILLS PRESS
132 Main Street
Erin, Ontario N0B 1T0, Canada
(519) 833-2407

Design by John Denison
Cartoons by Brian Fray
Cover photos by Ben Fischler
Typeset by Convertype, Toronto
Printed by Ampersand, Guelph

American Association
for State and Local History
Award of Merit

Winners of the
Heritage Canada
Communications Award

— CONTENTS —

SECTION I — BEGINNINGS

CHAPTER 1:	The Roots of the Railroad	— 9
CHAPTER 2:	The Network Expands and Develops	— 15
CHAPTER 3:	The Great Bicycle-Long Island Rail Road Race	— 23
CHAPTER 4:	This Means War!	— 27
CHAPTER 5:	Commuting in the 19th Century — Only for the Hardy	— 31
CHAPTER 6:	About Locomotives and Passenger Cars	— 39

SECTION II — INTO THE 20th CENTURY

CHAPTER 7:	The Big Switch — From Steam to Electricity	— 45
CHAPTER 8:	The Hudson Tubes	— 49
CHAPTER 9:	Tunnels, a Super Bridge and a Mammoth Terminal	— 65
CHAPTER 10:	Grand Central Terminal	— 73

SECTION III — DISASTERS

CHAPTER 11:	New York and New Haven Railroad, May 6, 1853	— 83
CHAPTER 12:	Double Disaster on the Long Island Rail Road, 1950	— 87
CHAPTER 13:	The Broker Derails	— 101
CHAPTER 14:	The Mystery of the Open Bridge	— 107

SECTION IV — ANATOMY OF A NETWORK

CHAPTER 15:	Reaching Into the New Era	— 115
CHAPTER 16:	The Decline and Fall of Practically Everybody	— 125
CHAPTER 17:	Rising From the Ashes	— 135
CHAPTER 18:	Stumbling Along With the LIRR	— 141
CHAPTER 19:	The Jersey Bounce	— 147

A Guide To Knowing and Enjoying the Tri-State Commuter Rail Lines	— 165
Postscript — Where Do We Go From Here?	— 173

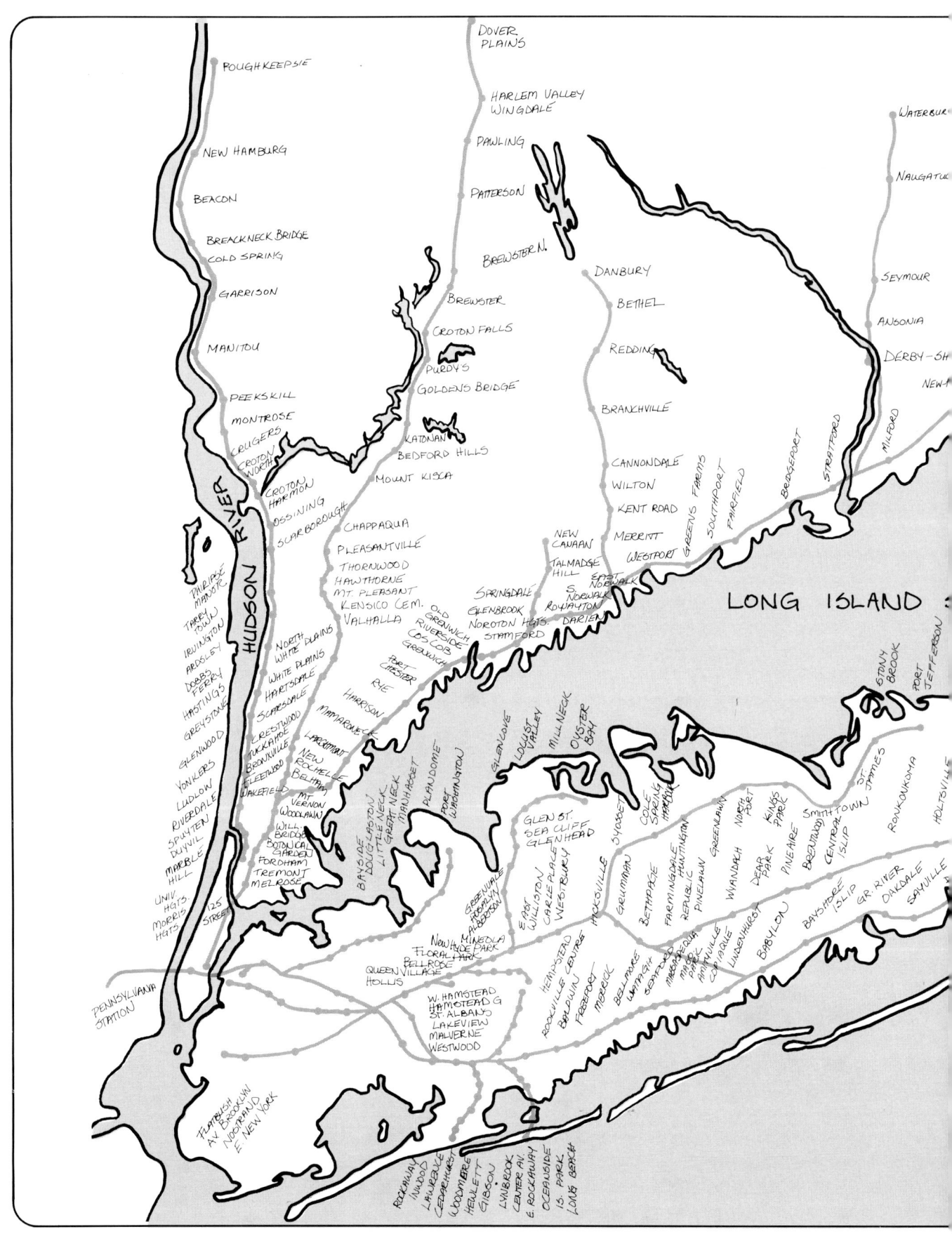

COMMUTER RAIL MAP

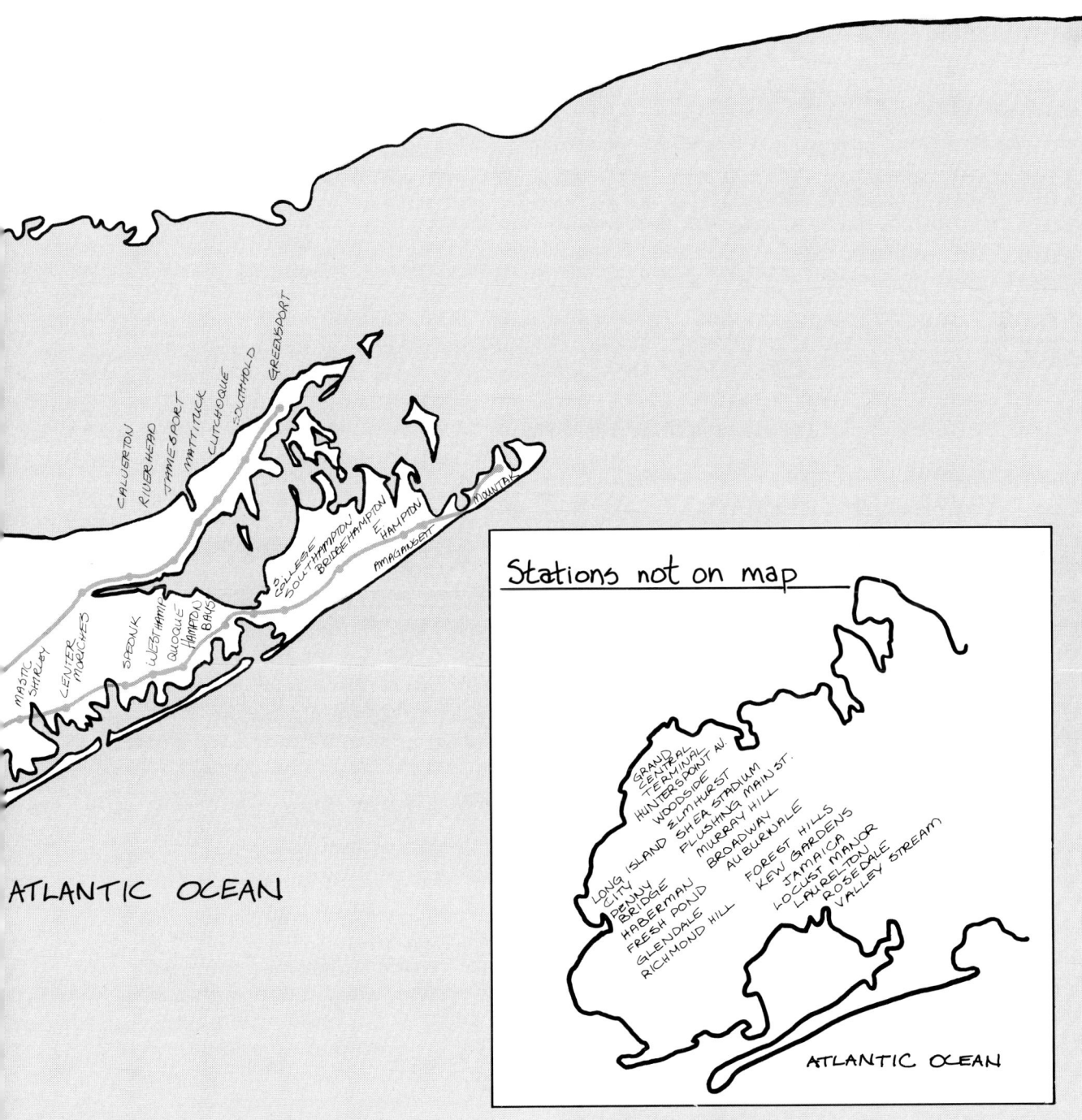

Earliest steam locomotive was little more than a horizontal boiler on wheels, pulling its water and fuel supply behind it. The engineer stood on an open platform. This engine and cars, built prior to 1820, qualifies as a "train" but not as a "railway" since there were no rails: the flat-rimmed wheels followed depressed ruts according to a system invented in Roman times.
— Stan Fischler Collection

SECTION I — BEGINNINGS

CHAPTER 1: THE ROOTS OF THE RAILROAD

Sitting in the White House, President Theodore Roosevelt read the telegraph message from New York City:

The first official train of the Hudson and Manhattan Railway Company under the Hudson River awaits your signal and your pleasure. W.G. McAdoo.

The mustachioed chief of state read the wire, broke into a wide grin, leaned forward and extended his right index finger to a white button sitting atop his desk. He pressed hard on the button, sending a current of electricity from Washington D.C. to a substation of The Hudson Tubes near the southern tip of Manhattan. There, underground, in a spanking new subway station at Sixth Avenue and West 19th Street, nine glistening pieces of rolling stock sat inert, their 60-volt, battery-powered emergency lights providing the only illumination.

Each car of the Hudson and Manhattan Railway bulged with notables, including Governors Charles Evans Hughes of New York State and Franklin Fort of New Jersey. Impatiently, William Gibbs McAdoo awaited the flow of the "juice." Then, within seconds of the Presidential push, the rows of bulbs hanging from the cars suddenly glowed and the rhythmic whine of the electric motor began.

"The tunneling of the Hudson River," said Roosevelt, "is indeed a notable achievement; one of those achievements of which all Americans are, as they should be, justly proud."

The underground link between Lower Manhattan and Hoboken was a project long-dreamed but never considered possible until late in the 19th century. As one of the inaugural passengers, 91-year-old John Bigelow, observed, anyone who had suggested in the middle of the 1800's that someday he might travel under the Hudson River in an electric train would have been tagged as "a lunatic."

Actually, the engineering accomplishment which resulted in regular New York-to-Hoboken commuter railroad service was long in coming. It was, in fact, appropriate that Hoboken be designated the end-of-track for the Hudson and Manhattan Railway Company because it was near the very site of the Hoboken station that the roots of commuter railroading were planted in the New York Metropolitan area.

The hero of the piece was Colonel John Stevens (for whom the Stevens Institute of Technology in Hoboken is named) who pioneered railroading after earlier successes in the field of transportation. Col. Stevens had established the world's first steam ferry in the Hudson River and his *Phoenix* had been the first steamboat to dare churn its way into the open sea. But when the Colonel proposed a railroad to cross New Jersey he was labelled a lunatic.

But men of Stevens' fibre are undaunted by the barbs of cynics. After a particularly arduous stagecoach ride from Trenton to Hoboken, Stevens vowed that there must be a better way to travel. Turnpikes, no matter how new, provided neither speed (for the merchant) nor comfort (for the traveller). Canals were fine and dandy — the Erie Canal being an example for Stevens — but they could not fulfill the promise implicit in the railroad.

"I can see nothing," wrote the Colonel, "to hinder a steam engine from moving with a velocity of 100 miles per hour. In practice, it may not be advisable to exceed 20 or 30 miles per hour, but I should not be surprised at seeing carriages propelled at 40 or 50." *Stevens' observations were made two years before English inventor George Stephenson had constructed his first locomotive.*

Stevens' analysis of transportation and its future prospects was astonishingly prophetic. "Rapid transportation," he noted, "would make the states one family intimately connected."

To prove his point, Stevens labored for months developing a comprehensive plan that would ultimately make railroads supercede canals as routes of commerce. The Colonel's railroad dream was articulated fully in 1811 in a collection of essays called "Documents Tending to Prove the Superior Advantages of Railway and Steam Carriages over Canal Navigation."

To convert his treatises into reality, Stevens made an appointment with the New Jersey Legislature. At the very least he expected a fair hearing, and for good reason. The Colonel had forged an excellent reputation in the Revolutionary War and was recognized as a successful inventor thanks to his experiments with steam engines. Better still, from a practical viewpoint, was the fact that a number of legislators were friends *and* relatives. What more could he ask for?

But Stevens' bid for a railroad charter was rebuked by the New Jersey Legislature. The reception to his proposals was like that which would greet those of a lunatic.

The rejection by New Jersey's Legislature, rather than deter Stevens, merely served to whet his competitive appetite. He accepted the obstacle but vowed to construct a practical detour — on paper.

If he could publish his documents in book form and get them to the public at large, perhaps opinion and, ultimately, the lawmakers could be swayed. So he had his "Documents" formally published and bound. He was taking his vision of a railroad to the people.

Perhaps the people would have been ready had their thoughts not been deflected by an urgent matter of survival. Great Britain once again was at war with the United States and more pressing matters were at hand. Patriotic to the core, Stevens shelved the railroad project and addressed himself to military matters. Realizing that firepower was a deficiency in the American arsenal, the Colonel devised a series of armor-piercing projectiles which, ironically, the conservative United States' military deemed too advanced to merit experimentation for the duration of the war.

Despite their rejection of Stevens' advanced munitions, the Americans prevailed and, by 1814, the Colonel pressed forward again in the hopes of selling the railroad plan to the American public. This time Stevens was the right man in the right place at the right time. The problem of transportation deficiencies had become all too evident during the war.

Stevens began laying out a proposed route for his railroad. Trekking through New Jersey, he became North America's original railroad surveyor, noting carefully in his journal the route his road would take to the state capitol at Trenton: ". . . the Devil's Brook, the Hide's Town road, and so to Princeton, up to Rowland's Tavern and the Ten Mile Stone; past the Quaker Wood by Jacob Haw's stable . . ." Interestingly, several of these projected railroad stops today are flourishing commuter stations.

Although he still lacked the motive power — it was only a year earlier, 1814, that George Stephenson had begun working on his first steam locomotive in England — Stevens applied for his railroad charter. This time, on February 6, 1815, he obtained a green light from the New Jersey Legislature, without any clear statement to the lawmakers that he intended to employ steam power.

With the state's approval, Stevens' next goal was the acquisition of substantial financial backing for the project. This would prove to be more difficult than he had anticipated. Several proposals to financiers were rebuffed. Not until the Colonel approached prominent New Yorker DeWitt Clinton did he receive a positive nibble.

While not exactly ecstatic about Stevens' suggestion to build a New York railroad, Clinton replied that he could see a future in steam-powered locomotives rolling on steel rails, *provided* that experiments being conducted in Great Britain proved successful. In his letter Clinton enclosed a newspaper story relating details of the British experiment. "If that succeeds," commented Clinton, "then there should be no difficulty in realizing your views!"

Stevens could not wait for another newspaper clipping to announce the success (or failure) of the English experiment. Where he had been spending considerable time in the board rooms of millionaire investors, the Colonel now camped in Hoboken. There he enthusiastically applied his wisdom to the wood and metal at hand, and in 1825 completed the first steam locomotive in the United States.

Now the Colonel was ready. With the finished steam engine before their eyes, investors would not be able to restrain themselves from backing his railroad concept. Dubbed the "Steam Waggon," Stevens' locomotive resembled a horseless wagon with two meshing gears atop and below the platform. The wheels were ordinary wooden wheels which would roll over wooden rails fortified with a thin strip of metal on top.

Fortunately for Stevens, his estate provided ample room for a definitive experiment. He laid out a 630-foot-long circular track, which included a center (third) rail serrated throughout so that the locomotive's (turning) lower gear could mesh with the track, thereby propelling the "Steam Waggon" around the grounds. For his riders, the Colonel added a pair of benches above and behind the rear wheels. Stevens astutely realized that some prospective investors would question the locomotive's ability to climb a hill. With this in mind, he banked a section of the track so that it climbed 30 inches and then dropped down again.

Once his engine was completed and personally tested, Stevens dispatched invitations. To his delight, he received several affirmative replies.

Black smoke spewed over "The Green" at Castle Point (now the site of Hoboken's City Hall) as the 16-foot "Steam Waggon" traversed the track at 12 miles per hour. Fearful though they were, passengers came away persuaded that the Colonel's contraption not only worked but did, in fact, possess excellent possibilities for transporting both people and parcels.

The natural result of Stevens' successful locomotive experiment was New Jersey's first railroad. Ironically, despite the Colonel's pioneer work, railroads were constructed in South Carolina, New York and Maryland before the Camden and Amboy Railroad was chartered in 1831.

Never did the pioneer betray bitterness that his dream took so long to develop. When the Camden and Amboy's first steam locomotive arrived in New Jersey in August 1831, the 82-year-old inventor pulled out all stops. Colonel John invited a veritable legion of friends and associates to a champagne party to herald the grand event: his spirits reportedly "as sparkling and abundant as the champagne." Apparently, Colonel John was not even perturbed that the new railroad failed to follow the route he had originally planned.

With Colonel John in retirement — actually he turned his attention to the creation of a New Jersey State University *to be financed from railroad taxes* — his sons, Robert L. and Edwin A., guided the Camden and Amboy to a position of eminence. Because of their father's efforts in laying the groundwork for railroading, public opinion had so been swayed that it required but ten minutes to sell $1,000,000 of stock in the Camden and Amboy when it was put up for sale. By contrast, a year was required to sell all the stock in the competing Delaware and Raritan Canal, which covered virtually the same route as the railroad.

Although he never quite obtained the acclaim directed at his father, Robert soon became as important an influence on railroading — modern as well as early — as any man who came down the pike. Curiously, some of his most significant insights developed while he was aboard the sailing ship *Hibernia* bound for Great Britain in 1830.

Stevens' mission was the purchase of vital supplies for the new line, particularly rails. Railroading was such a new industry in the United States that necessary supplies were scarce. Rails at that time were nothing more than lengths of iron strapped on top of wooden planks. But few iron works had opened in America and there was none of the advanced technology that had enabled the British to develop a stronger, standard rail. Stevens pondered the problem of producing a completely different rail, one which ultimately could be developed at home and would be strong and durable enough to cope with the bitter winters the Camden and Amboy would ultimately encounter. He worked the problem out in his head, then borrowed a chunk of lumber from the ship's carpenter and carved out his design. The result was the *T-rail*, essentially the same style used today throughout the world. With knife in hand and more wood available, Stevens then carved out the *fish plate* on which the rail sits and is spiked secure.

Stevens visited several English mills in the hopes of locating one that would produce his *T-rail*, but the conservative British rejected his idea as potentially damaging to their equipment. As tenacious as his father had been, Robert decided to try his luck in Wales, where his father had an old friend in the mill business. At first the Welshman was wary, but a deal was made when Robert promised to pay damages, should any occur. Soon the rails came out of the rollers, although not exactly as Stevens had hoped.

Instead of coming out straight, as rails should, the new product was warped, threatening to invalidate Stevens' blueprint before he could even test it back home. Again the persistence which characterized the family paid off. Stevens — aided by the manufacturer — went back to the drawing board and came up with a suggestion for straightening the rails while still hot. The 16-foot, 36-pound rails then came out as anticipated.

Robert then visited with the English locomotive inventor, George Stephenson, who was producing and test-operating a brand new "steam wagon" called *Planet*. Stevens liked what he saw of the vehicle and promptly ordered an identical model for the Camden and Amboy, which would be known as *John Bull*.

When *John Bull* made its American debut in August of 1831, the crowd that came out to see the iron horse instead saw nothing but wood! *John Bull* was nothing more than a kit! There was no locomotive as such, just a collection of wooden crates containing the various parts of the locomotive.

Apparently the British manufacturer either forgot to include instructions, or assumed that the ingenious Americans would put the pieces together unaided, for there were no diagrams, blueprints or instructions whatsoever. Fortunately Stevens had employed a young man named Isaac Dripps, who not only was willing but able to construct the ten-ton engine from scratch. By November the 22-year-old Dripps had completed the locomotive.

Ever the optimist, Robert Stevens prepared a victory banquet to celebrate the successful world premiere run of *John Bull* on November 12, 1831. Isaac Dripps and his fireman, Ben Higgins, were engulfed by a throng which was, in turn, frightened, curious, expectant and — except for those who favored canal transport — extremely hopeful.

Behind Dripps and Higgins in *John Bull* sat a clutch of dignitaries and potential investors, all jammed in fragile-looking coaches. When the moment arrived, fireman Higgins flung pieces of pine wood into the maw of the firebox. A blaze developed and Dripps awaited the precious moment when the steam scale would reach 30 pounds — the signal that he could open the throttle.

Sure enough, the hissing, belching monster began to cough smoke and then, better still, lurch forward. Dripps not only had constructed the *John Bull*, but now, as all of Bordentown, New Jersey, stared in awe and appreciation, he got the thing to move. So successful was this maiden run that dozens of onlookers who had been previously skeptical or frightened now clamored for a ride. Stevens graciously welcomed them, including the first female passenger, one Madame Murat, wife of Prince Murat and niece, by marriage, to Napoleon. In addition, a collection of journalists was on hand to chronicle the event. Raves were the order of the day.

The *New Jersey Gazette* noted that the locomotive pulled the train "with great velocity." The men who counted, politicians and investors, liked what they saw, and liked even more what they heard: *John Bull* would be able to chug a mile in 120 seconds, if not less.

Such enthusiasm spurred construction. Stones for the roadbed — wooden ties were not yet in vogue — were obtained from, of all places, Sing Sing prison. Unfortunately for Stevens, the inmates could not produce stones as fast as he wanted the railroad line lengthened. It was Robert's aim to push the line through to Amboy by the winter of 1832. When it became apparent that the Sing Sing shipments would be too slow for the target date, Stevens again resorted to creative thinking, once more producing a railroad innovation.

Since he couldn't get the flat stones quickly enough, Stevens decided to mount the rails on logs placed like a horizontal ladder along the proposed route. To keep the rails in place, Stevens then ordered his crews to place a mound of broken rock around the logs every few feet. And so the modern railbed came into being!

Another problem — the *John Bull's* short wheelbase caused it to derail on curves — led to yet another American railroad innovation: the cowcatcher. When Stevens and Dripps devised the cowcatcher, it was meant to serve solely as an extension of the locomotive, with two pilot wheels to prevent derailment. However, its value in nudging obstacles, including cows, out of the way soon became obvious. Thus the "cow-catcher" got its name and its long-term usage.

Passenger revenues grew and soon freight revenue burgeoned as well, for in January 1833 freight carriers were added to the line. By the end of that year Stevens had no less than three new locomotives under construction — not in Great Britain, but in Hoboken, since the prototype was constructed from designs produced by Robert Stevens and Isaac Dripps. The second locomotive was completed in 1834, and the 30-tonner was immediately dubbed *Monster*.

More than 100,000 passengers rode the Camden and Amboy in its first year. Five years later the annual rate exceeded 160,000 riders. Centers not included in the original route clamored for recognition from the Camden and Amboy and, sensibly, the directors responded by extending the railroad to larger towns.

By 1839, when Colonel John Stevens died, enough railroads were snaking through New Jersey for the distinguished inventor to go to his resting place secure in the knowledge that he had fathered a great industry.

"In the course of these discussions the railroad officials would produce flasks of vintage whiskey."

CHAPTER 2: THE NETWORK EXPANDS AND DEVELOPS

While Colonel John Stevens and his sons were laying the groundwork for railroading in New Jersey, a group of New Yorkers moved ahead with plans for steam-powered train service on Manhattan Island. Surely New York soon would require what amounted to a commuter rail line. The metropolis was growing faster than any community in New Jersey or Connecticut, counting more than 200,000 citizens by 1831, when the New York and Harlem Railroad Company received its charter from the New York State Legislature.

According to the charter, the "city" end of the commuter line would terminate at 23rd Street between Third and Eighth avenues (depending upon the site selected by the railroad planners). The "suburban" terminus would be the village of Harlem, then a distant six-and-a-half miles away from the bustle of America's biggest city. Like any good commuter line, the New York and Harlem also would serve a burgeoning town in between, in this case Yorkville.

Since the steam locomotive had yet to become popular in North America, supporters of the New York and Harlem agreed that the trains would be horse-drawn (as they had been originally in New Jersey).

With the charter and funds in hand, the go-ahead for construction was given in 1832, and on February 23rd of that year the first shovelful of dirt was tossed. Before the snows of winter had arrived, horsecars were plying a route along The Bowery (that section of Manhattan now known as Fourth Avenue) between Prince Street and 14th Street at what is now Union Square.

There is some question as to whether it would be appropriate to call the line, as it ran then, a legitimate railroad. "In reality," according to traction expert William D. Middleton, "this first section of the New York and Harlem was no more than a streetcar line; indeed its opening is celebrated as the first American street railway."

But the horse-drawn carriages *did* roll on rails, and as far as those New Yorkers who showed up for the inital run on November 14, 1832, were concerned, their latest transportation venture *was* a railroad. That is precisely what the city's *Morning Courier and Enquirer* called it after covering the inaugural run. The newspaper predicted that the New York and Harlem would — as any good commuter line ultimately did — provide a practical link between urban employment and suburban living, so that New Yorkers could enjoy landowning with "a garden, orchard, dairy and other conveniences." In its report of the opening day proceedings the *Morning Courier and Enquirer* observed:

"The Harlem Railroad Company with the Mayor, Corporation, and strangers of distinction, left the City Hall in carriages to the place of the depot near Union Square, where two splendid cars made by Milne Parker, each with two horses, were in waiting.

"These cars are made low with broad iron wheels which fit the flanges of the railroad after an improved model from the Liverpool and Manchester cars. They resemble an omnibus, or rather several omnibuses attached to each other, padded with fine cloth and handsome glass windows, each capable of containing outside and inside, fully forty passengers. The company was soon seated and the horses trotted off in handsome style, with great ease, at the rate of about twelve miles, followed by a number of private barouches and horsemen. Groups of spectators greeted the passengers of the cars with shouts and every window of the Bowery was filled.

"After the experiment, the company and guests dined at the City Hall and terminated, in a very agreeable manner, the first essay of New Yorkers on a railroad in their own city."

Directors of the New York and Harlem perceived immediately that they had miscalculated in accepting 23rd Street as the southern terminus. A location closer to the heart of the city was needed, so permission to run the line as far south as Prince Street was sought and obtained.

Within five years of the first spade-turning, the New York and Harlem had proven worthy of its name; service between Lower Manhattan and 125th Street (Harlem) was launched in 1837 and proved so profitable that directors approved the opening of a second track to handle the volume of traffic. Meanwhile, the railroad opened a combined office and stable area at Fourth Avenue between 26th and 27th streets and erected a new southern terminus at Tryon Row in 1839, at what is now City Hall. It was only a matter of time before steam locomotives would roar up and down the bustling island. When steam did come, before 1840, the city fathers anticipated the problems that the noisy vehicles would bring, strictly limiting the operation of steam locomotion to the area *north* of 14th Street.

As steam became the accepted and predominant motive power, the New York and Harlem built, in the area where the office-stable complex was situated, a station to house the engines and serve as the southern terminal for all operations. By all indications, railroading could expect rapid growth in New York. Already the Camden and Amboy had extended its tentacles across New Jersey, and in 1840 the first train ran through from Jersey City to Philadelphia. Directors of the New York and Harlem were aware of the progress being made across the Hudson, as they were aware of the potential for passenger and freight traffic *north* of their Harlem end-of-track. There was, of course, plenty of exploitable New York State beyond, not to mention Connecticut to the northeast.

Attempts to strike out in the direction of Westchester County and points north had been made in the early 1830's. One of the most ambitious sets of blueprints was put together by backers of a New York and Albany Railroad. This proposed line obtained a charter in 1832, but never got on the track. Within a decade the now-burgeoning New York and Harlem seized the initiative missed by the New York and Albany and had its charter amended so that it could lay tracks beyond Harlem.

By 1841 commuters could travel from lower Manhattan to Fordham, in what is now the Bronx. Three years later the line was extended ambitiously into White Plains, hub of Westchester County. Onward and northward the pickaxes and hammers sounded their notes of railroad progress. A milestone was achieved in 1852 when the New York and Harlem reached the site of what is now the town of Chatham, New York, also a junction of the formidable Western Railroad of Massachusetts. Most gratifying to directors of the New York and Harlem was the continual increase in commuter traffic. The rapid development of communities in the Bronx was very much the result of accessibility provided by the railroad.

The New York and Harlem covered considerable mileage when it finally linked with the state capital in Albany, but did not include Connecticut in its domain. Other promoters realized that the void had to be filled, and in 1844 the New York and New Haven Railroad received it charter. The grand plan was not simply to connect the center of Manhattan with New Haven, but ultimately to press on to the hub of Massachusetts, Boston.

The New York and Harlem did not welcome the upstart New York and New Haven. When the new railroad made a bid to have its tracks enter New York City, the *original* line determinedly opposed the bid and had enough clout in the New York Legislature to defeat its quasi-competitor. As a result, the New York and New Haven had no choice but to enter negotiations with the New York and Harlem for the use of its tracks from Westchester (Mount Vernon) into the 27th Street station in Manhattan. Actually, the New Haven passengers were able to go all the way south to Canal Street, near Broadway, where the line had established its own station, but as in the case of the Harlem, the cars had to be towed by horses south of the 27th station. Whatever hostility existed between the two lines ultimately was resolved when, in 1857, they combined their passenger stations into a new building erected shoulder-to-shoulder on Fourth Avenue between 26th and 27th streets.

The combined Harlem and New Haven station became New York's first legitimate commuter terminal and the predecessor of today's goliath Grand Central Terminal. In his history of *Grand Central*, William Middleton vividly describes the scene at the Madison Square (the station was just north of Madison Square Terminal):

"Tracks (12) led in from Fourth Avenue between the two nearly identical station buildings. Twin columns, standing about 25 feet high midway on the Fourth Avenue front, marked the boundary between the tracks of the two railroad companies. An architrave resting atop these twin columns extended above gates on either side, supported by single columns at its opposite ends. The gates, which were raised to give passage to arriving and departing trains, were intended to help restrict entry to the train yard to only those holding tickets. This arrangement caused some complaint from those coming to see friends off, but the railroads allowed that 'the fine saloons of the depot afforded the best and most suitable facilities for shaking hands and the exchange of more affectionate adieus'."

The station (which ultimately became New York City's first Madison Square Garden) did a thriving business, serving more than 7,500 passengers daily. Between them, the Harlem and New Haven generated more than 30 trains both coming and going each day. Unfortunately for both lines the flourishing traffic also produced debits, particularly noise and pollution produced by the ever-growing number of locomotives. In 1844 the city fathers voted that steam locomotives no longer could operate below 32nd Street. In 1858 they set the limit at a terminal above 42nd Street. Nevertheless, the railroad cars could still reach southern Manhattan thanks to the teams of dependable horses that pulled the rolling stock downtown.

While the Harlem and New Haven continued to expand operations, another challenger entered the railroad market. The newcomer was expected to fail at first, but lived to become one of the greatest operations in the industry, the New York Central. In its infancy it was known as the Hudson River Railroad. Pessimists wrote obituaries in advance. "It can't compete with the Hudson River steamboats," they argued, pointing out that no less than five robust steamboat lines operated vessels between New York City and Albany. The New York and Harlem had kept this in mind when it originally laid out its route, deciding not to build tracks near the Hudson River communities so well served by the boats.

The doubting Thomases failed to consider the frigid New York State winters, which often immobilized boat traffic on the Hudson River from December through March. Centers of commerce such as Kingston, Croton and Poughkeepsie wanted to continue trading even when the Hudson was frozen. The natural answer was a railroad, and in 1849 the Hudson River Railroad linked Manhattan with Poughkeepsie. It began at a Manhattan station on 31st Street and within two years extended its tracks to Albany. Like the other two lines, the Hudson River Railroad was obliged to service the southern area of Manhattan and did so by means of horse teams drawing the trains along Tenth Avenue as far south as Chambers Street and West Broadway. As the Hudson River Railroad thrived it also expanded its operation. In 1861 it completed a new terminal at Tenth Avenue and 30th Street. President Abraham Lincoln stopped there enroute to Washington, D.C., from Springfield, Illinois, for his inauguration. Ironically, the same station was the scene of mourning on April 25, 1865, when Lincoln's funeral train carried his body from New York City (arriving first in Jersey City from Washington and then ferrying across the Hudson River) to his burial site in Springfield. When Lincoln arrived in Manhattan for the inauguration, his train was pulled by the locomotive *Union*, the same locomotive employed to power the funeral train back to Illinois.

By this time Colonel John Stevens' experiments with steam locomotion seemed a distant memory. Railroads were the only way to travel, as rapidly expanding America continued to move westward. As fast as the New York lines built rails west, so too did those in New Jersey. These were the lines which would comprise the vast network of commuter railroads serving the metropolitan area in the 20th century.

Naturally, the Camden and Amboy at first fought potential competitors with ruthless zeal, but it had no more chance of stopping their creation than of throwing back the Atlantic Ocean. In January 1831, New Jersey's second railroad charter was granted to the Paterson and Hudson River line. An excellent twosome, William Gibbs McNeill and George Washington Whistler, were hired to lay out the railroad's route. (As things happened Whistler married McNeill's sister, and their son, James Abbott McNeill Whistler, forever immortalized the marriage with a painting of Mother, ergo: Whistler's Mother!) McNeill and Whistler first linked Paterson with Aquackanonk (Passaic), and in June 1832 a team of horses pulled three double-decker cars over the tracks.

Meanwhile, still another group of Jerseyites, impressed with the Stevens' enterprise as well as the McNeill-Whistler project, decided that a railroad connecting Jersey City and Trenton through Newark would be useful. This presented a major engineering problem, namely the fording of New Jersey's marshy meadows. An equally formidable problem would be objections raised by the Camden and Amboy which did, in fact, stall its proposed competitor in the New Jersey Legislature. However, a good deal of wheeling and dealing on both sides eventually won the New Jersey Railroad and Transportation Company the third charter for a railroad in the state. The key clause that brought about the agreement was the new line's concession to the Camden and Amboy to run only to New Brunswick by way of Newark, Elizabethtown and Rahway. The Camden and Amboy was awarded a closer entrance to New York harbor, which virtually guaranteed that the new line would in no way slice into the profit of the Stevens' railroad.

Once the obstacles were disposed of, engineers set about the business of analyzing just how and where they would solve the three geographic obstacles of Bergen Hill, the Meadowlands and a pair of substantial rivers — the Hackensack and the Passaic.

Bergen Hill forms a natural wall separating both Paterson and Newark from Jersey City. In the 1830's there were no steam engines capable of climbing it, which meant that a deep cut through the hill would be necessary. The marshy meadowlands produced a different problem, as they were often covered with tidewater.

Taming the Passaic and Hackensack rivers proved to be the least demanding challenge. The Paterson and Hudson Railroad completed two substantial drawbridges — believed to be the first railroad drawbridges ever constructed — to the cheers of all Jerseyites. It was not as easy for the New Jersey Railroad. There was a Hackensack and Passaic Bridge Company with exclusive bridge rights to the area through which that line would run. The railroad had to buy out the company.

The Meadowlands at first appeared conquerable without too many problems. Engineers suggested that the railroad could be built by sinking piles into the marsh and then laying the tracks on top of them. But the Meadowlands did not cooperate and a new plan was necessary. A fill of thousands of great cedars and countless tons of dirt was made as a base. This fill then had to be allowed to settle for a year before the trains were allowed to roll.

This left the Bergen Hill. Both the Paterson and Hudson River Railroad and the New Jersey Railroad and Transportation Company would have liked to handle the project independently, but it seemed so formidable a project that they finally combined forces. The Paterson and Hudson paid two-fifths of the cost, while the New Jersey handled the rest. While this monumental engineering work awaited completion, passengers were carried over Bergen Hill in horse-drawn cars. The cut was completed (near the site of Journal Square in Jersey City) in 1838. Within two years traffic between Newark and Jersey City numbered 5,000 passengers weekly.

Many of these passengers were wary of the fire-belching machines that pulled the carriages, and a sufficient number expressed fright in the early days to persuade the directors that horse-drawn cars should provide supplementary service for the faint at heart. As for the courageous early passengers, they generally regarded their trip as something of an adventure. If, by chance, the rolling stock failed to negotiate a curve and jumped the track (a relatively common occurrence) riders would think nothing of helping the crew lift the lightweight carriages back on the rails. If the mishap happened to occur in the Meadowlands, the paying customers were permitted extra time to join the engineer and firemen in pursuit of snapping turtles!

Cooperation of a sort existed between the lines, especially when there existed an opportunity for profitable connections. Thus, the New Jersey Railroad and Transportation Company permitted the Camden and Amboy to use its tracks enroute to New York (and subsequently the Morris and Essex and the Jersey Central) while the Paterson and Hudson River line provided a vital Jersey City connection for the Erie Railroad.

"Thus the network spread," noted John T. Cunningham in his *Railroading In New Jersey*. "Towns grew along the way, industries expanded. New York businessmen began thinking of settling out in the beautiful state west of the Hudson. The commuter was about to be born."

This was true to a certain extent on the eastern side of the Hudson as well, where New Yorkers, more and more, began casting their eyes on development of Long Island, with its natural beaches on the Atlantic Ocean.

A primary attraction of a rail line there was the possibility of linkage with Boston via ship service from the north fork of Long Island. In the early 1830's these plans began to jell thanks, in large part, to the foresight of Major D.B. Douglass, chief engineer of the Brooklyn and Jamaica Railroad Company, which was incorporated in 1832. This pioneering line meandered through the village of Bedford (Brooklyn) and eastward through farmland to East New York. Douglass realized that the New York-to-Boston boat trip consumed 16 or more hours. A train-boat run to Boston, he estimated, could be made in as little as 11 hours. As a result of his projections, the Long Island Rail Road Company won its charter from the New York State Legislature on April 24, 1834. It would utilize the rails of the still incomplete Brooklyn and Jamaica (by leasing the B&J) and then add track to the very tip of Long Island.

The Brooklyn and Jamaica was finished in 1836 and, as promised, the Long Island leased the ten miles of trackage. From Jamaica, the Long Island Rail Road — according to its planners — would bisect central Suffolk County ignoring both the towns of the north and south shores. Serving Boston with high-speed expresses seemed more important than dealing with the farmers of Long Island. The Brooklyn and Jamaica, meanwhile, proved a helpful catalyst to the Long Island Rail Road, for not only did the B&J provide trackage for the LIRR, it also allowed the new line to operate Brooklyn and Jamaica locomotives.

By March 1837 construction crews of the Long Island had hammered their way eastward to the site of what is now Hicksville. Only one hamlet of any consequence was situated between Hicksville and Jamaica, that being Brushville, now the thriving community of Queens Village. Hicksville, named for Valentine Hicks, second president of the new railroad, became the first of several towns to be born along the railroad's trackage. It was soon a respectable-sized community.

LIRR chroniclers Ron Ziel and George Foster recount the ploy used by Long Island track planners to eliminate grade crossings: "The railroad management frequently arranged meetings with the town fathers of on-line villages, ostensibly for the purpose of solving any problems that might threaten to interfere with the orderly passage of the steamcars. In the course of these discussions the railroad officials would produce flasks of vintage whiskey. In due time, when the elected protectors of the people's interests were thoroughly inebriated, the railroad officers would persuade them to sign legal documents permitting the LIRR to cross existing roads, thus closing the roads to all traffic. Many of these roads are still in existence, with the railroad's embankment bisecting them right in the middle of the towns."

In order to speed completion of the Long Island Rail Road, two separate track gangs were utilized; one operating from the east, moving westward, and the other going in the opposite direction. That the LIRR directors aimed for the high quality marked by the early New Jersey lines was evident in the rail purchased in Liverpool, England. Weighing 55 pounds per yard, the rail was delivered on a regular basis, until one day a group of Irish-born track-layers ran out of the English rail within two miles of their targeted end-of-track. Rather than sit back and await the next shipment — one could never be sure when deliveries would be made — the Irishmen produced an ersatz track by first felling heavy timbers and then using them as the base for rails which were no more than strap iron attached to the timbers. Despite this crude arrangement, the trains were able to negotiate this temporary spread of track until the real stuff arrived from Great Britain.

Douglass had predicted that the trip from Brooklyn to Greenport, the eastern terminus, would take some five hours. Imagine his surprise when, after track work was completed, three Long Island Rail Road trains delivered their excursion passengers from Brooklyn to Greenport in three-and-a-half hours, on July 27, 1844. What would become known as "The Route of the Dashing Commuter" was now in business, for better or worse!

On the plus side was the indisputable fact that a major railroad now crossed burgeoning Long Island, promising grand transportation possibilities in terms of a New York-New England coupling. On the minus side there was a series of episodes which were to become symbolic of the Long Island Rail Road's 20th century image as the indifferent railroad.

The railroad's high command erred in its policy toward native Long Islanders. The first mistake was giving the fast-trip-to-Boston higher priority than connections with major Long Island towns. The second *faux pas* was a generally officious attitude toward the locals, which soon aroused their wrath.

To a rational, objective observer, it would seem that Long Islanders would have welcomed the railroad in the manner that New Jerseyites did the Camden and Amboy and those lines that immediately followed. But the residents of Nassau and Suffolk, to a large extent, viewed the railroad as a callous interloper which, among other things, was running down their cattle and setting fire to the countryside with burning cinders which spewed from the locomotives. Long Islanders resorted to sabotaging the right-of-way and burning down stations. Wherever possible the railroad hired police to guard against the guerilla attacks, but these often proved futile since the railroad cops, mostly hired from the same Long Island community from whence the saboteurs came, merely turned away when the attacks hit.

As Ziel and Foster noted, a number of trains were wrecked by the Long Island guerilla fighters and "in one memorable episode, an escort engine fell through the Peconic River bridge after some Riverhead folk sawed through the timbers."

An article in the *Long Island Forum* recorded the monologue of a Long Island boy who was scared out of his wits when he encountered his first train at Manorville:

"I tramped along at a pretty lively gait and reached the track fust one. There wasn't no train nur nothin' in sight, so I set down t'wait and musta fell asleep. Fust thing I knew, I heard thunderin'; so I jumped up and seen the sun was shinin' bright's could be. Then I got out on the track and thar she was comin'. I just stood there and looked and she kep' a'comin' and a'comin'; and fust thing I knew, she let out a squeal. That scairt me, so I turned and run and kep' a'comin' right after me, a squealin' at every jump. She kep' on chasin' me fur pretty nigh a half a mile, an' she never gained on me much; but I was beginnin' to git het up and a mite winded, so I th't mebbe I could jump down the bank a'fore she could ketch me, and so I did; but she never gained on me but just a mite."

The callousness of the railroad continually provoked the natives into some form of retribution or another. An elderly lady who suffered the indignity of first losing her cow in a confrontation with a Long Island Rail Road locomotive was then told the company would not compensate her for the loss of the animal.

With that, the lady came up with a delicious form of revenge. Each day she would amble over to a section of track near her farm where the locomotive negotiated a perceptible grade. Under ordinary conditions this presented no problem to the engineer, but the furious woman changed all that by hauling a large amount of soap, then rubbing it onto the tracks. The rails now were made slippery as they could be and then, with the addition of a bit of water, even slipperier. That done, the lady would repair to a convenient vantage point to await the arrival of the next train. At last the locomotive would come into view and begin negotiating the grade, but once the driving wheels reached the super-lubricated rails, all traction was lost. The goliath locomotive was stalled until help could be obtained. Day after day the irate woman repeated her ritual. Frustrated and furious, the railroad's directors finally reached into their safe to produce $20 for the lost cow and, from then on, the woman's soap was confined to the kitchen and bathroom.

When residents of Manorville tried to force the railroad to foot half of the bill for lost livestock, the LIRR decided to have *its engineers* pick up part of the tab for any cows, bulls, pigs or chickens mowed down by the steam engines.

The success of the Long Island Rail Road as a commercial enterprise was predicated on an engineering study completed in the early 1830's, which stated that it would be virtually impossible to extend a railroad from New York City to Boston, via southern Connecticut, because of the supposedly impassible marshland, tributaries, rivers and hills beyond Westchester County in Connecticut. For six years, the LIRR enjoyed the fruits of the train-boat connection to Boston, but by 1850 the bubble burst. Engineers and construction workers devised the means of overcoming southern Connecticut's natural obstacles, extending tracks from New York to Boston. With that, the Long Island, much to its directors' dismay, became "just" a commuter railroad.

CHAPTER 3: THE GREAT BICYCLE-LONG ISLAND RAIL ROAD RACE

The Long Island Rail Road, America's most abused commuter line, never was more embarrassed than on a clear, cool June morning in 1898 when a Brooklyn cyclist won a race against the railroad's speediest locomotive.

Charles N. Murphy, a New York City policeman and amateur bicycle racer, delivered the humiliation, but it was the Long Island Rail Road that actually suggested the race. The idea was the brainchild of Hal Fullerton, an official of the LIRR's passenger department, who had heard Murphy boast that he could keep pace with any railroad locomotive in the world.

Fullerton had a keen sense of publicity and asked Murphy whether he would be willing to cover a three-mile distance pedalling against a high-speed locomotive. "I'll ride on any track that's available," said Murphy. "All I need is a shield to cut down wind resistance that will develop when the train picks up speed."

Fullerton ordered the railroad's best engineers to study the problem of constructing a bicycle track along the road bed. A prerequisite was a section that would be smooth, level, and straight. "We examined miles and miles of track," said Fullerton, "and finally found a section at Maywood, Long Island, that seemed to fill the requirements as perfectly as possible."

Flanked by bushes and weeds, the track there was a level three miles long. Railroad engineers believed a speed of 60 miles per hour would be more than enough for the locomotive to outrace Murphy, so they tested the engines to determine how long a distance was necessary for the locomotive to reach that speed. At the time the LIRR was a burgeoning, high-speed operation with some of the newest and fastest rolling stock on the continent. Fullerton was advised that any one of a dozen engines could do the job.

Meanwhile, the 29-year-old Murphy had gone into training. His plan as well was to reach a speed of 60 m.p.h., something no human had ever achieved on a bicycle.

"As soon as I started my workouts and told people what I was up to," said Murphy, "I immediately became the laughingstock of the world — and particularly in my own precinct house."

After considering several possibilities, the railroad's engineers finally devised a special track for the bicycle. Wooden planks were firmly secured in a lateral position between the rails to act as a base. Then, five 10-inch boards were placed side-by-side lengthwise so that the railroad bed was converted into a wooden pathway.

A slim blond who wore a mustache, Murphy demanded a wind shield be built on the rear of the train's lone passenger car to create dead air behind the train. Without such a device, Murphy could slip into violent air currents generated by the speeding locomotive and be blown off the track. The LIRR constructed a hood from track level to roof level, projecting 11 feet four inches from the back of the passenger coach.

Murphy approved of the hood, but allowed that he feared the locomotive might vary its speed. Sudden deceleration could result in the cyclist plowing headlong into the windbreak. To prevent such a disaster Fullerton ordered a trial run on June 29, 1898, one day before the race.

Sam Booth, the locomotive engineer, was given instructions to cover the trial mile in one minute and 25 seconds. He revved up the engines while Murphy crouched within the three-sided wooden hood, got the signal and started the train. Murphy pedalled easily as the locomotive gained momentum. He never strayed from the ten-inch-wide middle plank and never dropped back as the train reached high speed. Murphy executed the trial run in 65 seconds — 20 seconds faster than planned. (Once the mile was completed he was hauled aboard the rear platform.)

"The reason that happened," Fullerton explained, "was because the engine gathered speed faster than we expected during the first quarter mile. The engineer wouldn't dare slow down on account of Murphy, so he kept going."

But that was only a test run, completely lacking the tension and hoopla that would accompany the "official" race the following day. Early on the morning of June 30th spectators began gathering in the fields along the tracks between Babylon and Bethpage. Having heard about his successful test run, onlookers already had nicknamed the New York cop "Mile-a-Minute Murphy."

He appeared at the starting line wearing a light blue racing jersey emblazoned with the emblem of the Tribune bicycle which he would ride. Having positioned himself behind the locomotive's single passenger car, Murphy placed a pair of goggles over his eyes and fixed a grotesque dust protector suggesting a gas mask over his nose and mouth.

The passenger car overflowed with reporters, trainers, railroad officials, four timekeepers and referee James Sullivan. Meanwhile, a mile away, peering nervously up the rails, was Murphy's young wife, cradling their little son in her arms.

After Murphy called, "I'm ready," to the judges, he crouched forward and focused his eyes on a strip of white wood nailed vertically from the platform as a guide-post to help him ride along the center of the track. A mile back from the starting line the engineer opened the throttle and the race was on. The locomotive was a good one and when it reached the starting line its speedometer recorded 60 miles per hour.

Murphy maintained a splendidly frantic pace as the locomotive thundered along the roadbed, but suddenly an unforeseen problem developed. The huge engine shook the roadbed so violently that the vibrations threatened to hurl Murphy clear of the tracks. Compounding the problem was the fact that small pieces of rubber from a roller sweeping the course ahead of the bicycle continually struck Murphy about the head and chest.

Nevertheless, he managed to keep pace with the locomotive as it passed the first quarter mark. But as Murphy approached the mid-point in the race he faltered and dropped 50 feet behind the railroad car. Spectators standing on the rear platform of the train implored Murphy to pedal harder, but his front wheel struck a loosened plank in the roadbed and wobbled perilously for a split second before Murphy regained control.

Then Murphy appeared to regain his confidence and his strength. As he headed for the three-quarter pole, Murphy relentlessly began moving closer to the train at a speed of better than a mile a minute.

Still, the hot rubber and cinders continued to bounce off his leg tights, some burning holes in his jersey. Oblivious to these hazards, Murphy pedalled even more vigorously and regained all the lost footage as he approached the American flag signalling the finish line. He rolled past the marker at the same speed as the train, having pedalled the mile in 57 4/5 seconds. He thus became the first man on a bicycle ever to cover a mile in less than a minute.

But Murphy's troubles weren't over. The locomotive braked more sharply than it had the previous day and the triumphant cyclist collided head-first with the platform. Fortunately, several observers had been leaning over the rear guardrails and managed to get their hands on the injured man. They hauled him aboard the train only to discover he was unconscious.

Murphy was carried to a cot inside the car, where doctors took his pulse. Before the race his pulse beat was 76 per minute and his temperature 98.4 degrees. Now his pulse rate was 84, up eight counts, and his temperature 99.5 degrees.

When Murphy regained consciousness a cheer went up inside the railroad car. Engineer Sam Booth burst into tears. "Murphy," he said, "to tell you the truth I thought I had lost you."

Murphy's speed record lasted for 42 years, until May 17, 1941, when Alfred "Alf" Letourner, a six-day bike racer, rode behind the windshield attached to the rear of Ronney Householder's racing car. Riding the highest-geared bicycle ever built, Letourner covered an officially measured mile in 33.05 seconds at the rate of 108.92 miles per hour.

This time, however, the Long Island Rail Road refrained from issuing a challenge.

One of the most bizarre stunts of the 19th century was the bicycle-steam engine race which pitted a New York cop, "Mile-A-Minute Murphy," against a crack LIRR steam engine, seen here being outfitted for the challenge. Note the wooden platform between the rails, built for Murphy's bike.
– Stan Fischler Collection

CHAPTER 4: THIS MEANS WAR!

The Long Island Rail Road's colossal mistake of not expecting competition via Connecticut was not matched in New Jersey. The Camden and Amboy took great care to establish its power in that state, their cleverest ploy being to sell the state 1,000 shares of stock in return for monopoly rights, with the understanding that if any competition developed they lost the stock.

Through the early 1840's the Camden and Amboy developed such power that judges and newspapers fearfully bowed to its wishes. Finally, in 1848, a political economist named Harry C. Carey, in a series of harsh letters to newspapers under the pseudonym "Citizen of Burlington", asserted that the Camden and Amboy was doing wrong by the state. Something should be done about it. The charges were so potent that even the traditionally acquiescent State Assembly mounted a high dudgeon and promised to look into the matter. But the first "investigation" was so feeble in its attempts to unearth wrongdoing that it was scrapped, and a second commission, which did find some evidence of hanky-panky, wrote it off as a bookkeeping error.

In effect the commission exonerated the Camden and Amboy, and this, in the eyes of the railroad, gave it *carte blanche* to wheel and deal with impunity. The Camden and Amboy cast its covetous eyes on the New Jersey Rail Road and Transportation Company which coupled between New Brunswick and Jersey City.

The Stevens' line had several weapons at its command. For one, Edward A. Stevens, treasurer of the Camden and Amboy, was now a powerful director of the Morris and Essex Rail Road connecting Newark and Dover, New Jersey. Further, the Hoboken Land and Improvement Company, run by the Stevens, had bid for a charter to construct a railroad to Newark to connect with the Morris and Essex. Officials of the New Jersey Rail Road and Transportation Company realized they were in the middle of a rapidly closing economic vise. Their attempts to lease the Morris and Essex were futile since Stevens virtually ruled the line. When the New Jersey Rail Road subsequently warned that it would construct a new line across the state, Camden and Amboy board members chuckled sardonically. They felt assured that it was *they* who held the clout in the legislature, where charters are granted. Each year the gallant New Jersey Rail Road fought and each year the Camden and Amboy flexed a larger muscle. At last, in 1867, the white flag was flown and the underdog consolidated with the Camden and Amboy and the Delaware and Raritan Canal, forming a joint company which controlled all traffic crossing New Jersey between New York and Philadelphia.

This was not the first war between New Jersey's railroads nor would it be the last. Earlier brushfires had developed between the Elizabethtown and Somerville Rail Road (chartered in 1831) and the Morris and Essex (chartered in 1835), which ultimately became the Jersey Central and the Lackawanna, respectively. After 28-year-old John Taylor Johnston became president of the Somerville and Easton Rail Road in 1848, he engineered a merger with the Elizabethtown and Somerville Rail Road in 1849 to form the Central Rail Road Company of New Jersey, known to intimates as the Jersey Central.

Johnston's Jersey Central pushed its way to the Delaware River in 1852; the Morris and Essex did so on 1865. Both were after the anthracite coal business just beyond. Jersey Central got there first and did grand business through the 1850's and into the 1860's. During the same period the Camden and Amboy was riding high, wide and handsome. Now the Jersey Central barons wanted a terminal in Jersey City across from Manhattan — they had been sending freight into Jersey City via the New Jersey Rail Road. A couple of problems needed to be cleared. To establish a Jersey City terminal, one had to find an appropriate location and, at that time, the only potential site consisted of the mud flats of South Cove, hardly a desirable spot. The other problem was finding a way of getting the trains across two-mile-wide Newark Bay.

As so often was the case in early railroad-building, those who voiced skepticism were soon ridiculed by the accomplishments of the optimists. Jersey Central engineers spanned the Bay with the longest bridge of its kind in the world, and in 1864 commuter trains were rolling on it. The Jersey City terminal project was just as difficult because of the tides and mud flats of South Cove.

John Taylor Johnston studied the area and produced a solution which would precipitate a war not unlike that between the Long Island Rail Road and the farmers of Nassau and Suffolk counties. While standing on the mud flats of Jersey City, an area populated by oyster planters and fishermen, Johnston looked across the Hudson River to New York City and turned to an aide: "Why can't we use the garbage of Manhattan to fill in the mud flats and then build the terminal on that?" It was a question which begged no reply.

Johnston arranged a deal whereby New York's garbage was towed across the Hudson to South Cove until the fill reached a point 1,000 feet into the river. But the malodorous nature of the fill sparked complaint after complaint from furious homeowners within smelling distance of South Cove. The burghers finally tired of protesting, and Johnston had his Jersey Central terminal. Another railroad had won a war against the landowners on whose acreage the tracks skirted.

More vicious were the wars between railroad and railroad. Among the more interesting was the clash between what ultimately would become two commuter giants — the Erie and the Lackawanna. The trouble dated back to the early 1860's when the Morris and Essex arrived at Hoboken via the Camden and Amboy branch line. His fingers in virtually every railroad pie, Stevens had provided financial assistance to the Erie when it decided to bore a tunnel through Bergen Hill, in exchange for allowing Morris and Essex trains to use it. The Morris and Essex was leased by the Lackawanna in 1868, but use of the tunnel caused no problems at first.

Nobody complained as long as the Morris and Essex trains came in from Morristown, but the Erie screamed bloody murder when the Boonton branch of the Lackawanna was constructed to Hoboken via Paterson in 1870. "The Erie," wrote New Jersey rail historian John T. Cunningham, "felt that to be a definite infringement of its Paterson territory; when the time came for a physical rail connection outside Bergen Tunnel, trouble flared. 'Prince Erie' — Jim Fisk — took matters into his hands early in December 1870. First he had a locomotive placed across the mouth of the tunnel and he brought 1,000 men to see that it wasn't moved. The fact that no Erie trains moved either was a matter of small moment to Fisk. As long as the Lackawanna trains were stopped 'Prince Erie' was happy."

The ensuing scene could have been excerpted from a Laurel and Hardy movie were it not of such serious nature to the participants involved, especially the commuters. When trains reached the blockade and were forced to stop, passengers alighted, demanding that the locomotive be removed. In no time at all word of the blockade reached the Governor's mansion.

More sensitive to the commuter's plight than most contemporary politicians, Governor Randolph sped to the scene and ordered the New Jersey militia to stand ready for action, if necessary. A man of direct action, the Governor then confronted railroad baron Fisk himself. "Take that locomotive off the tracks," Randolph demanded. You're holding up the mails. If you don't I'll take possession in the name of the state." Then, a threatening pause: "And I have the New Jersey militia to back me up!"

Fisk took the prudent course and ordered the locomotive removed, but he wasn't through harassing the Lackawanna. If he couldn't actually shut the tunnel Fisk could slow down enemy trains enough to force the Lackawanna to re-think its policies; and that is precisely what happened. After sufficient harassment by the Erie, directors of the Lackawanna convened and agreed that it would be less trouble for the line to build its own tunnel through Bergen Hill than to put up with the Erie's interminable troublemaking. Begun in 1874, the Lackawanna tunnel was completed two years later, thus ending another railway battle.

In that same year another war brewed between the Delaware and Bound Brook Railroad and the Pennsylvania Railroad. Known as "the Hopewell Frog War," it developed after the Delaware and Bound Brook began laying tracks from Jenkintown, Pennsylvania, to link with the Jersey Central at Bound Brook, New Jersey, a move which would lead to formation of the Reading Railroad. The problem was that the Delaware and Bound Brook's line crossed the tracks of the Mercer and Somerset, an affiliate of the larger Pennsylvania line.

In situations such as these, railroads have the option of either constructing a trestle over the existing track or, as in this case, installing a *frog*, which is nothing more than a crossover track which allows trains of both lines to cross over the other railroad's track without derailment.

When the Pennsylvania (Mercer and Somerset) got wind of the fact that the Delaware and Bound Brook was preparing to send out a track gang to Hopewell to install a frog, the order went out to stop the frog-laying at all costs. To do so Pennsy officials ordered that a locomotive be placed on the tracks in the precise spot where the Delaware and Bound Brook line would cross the Mercer and Somerset.

On the night of December 5, 1876, a blockading Mercer and Somerset locomotive was forced to retreat temporarily to a siding in order to permit a main line train to pass through. Alertly, the Delaware and Bound Brook dispatched 200 workers to the scene, where they promptly chained the Mercer and Somerset to the siding. That done, they fortified the tracks so that no interference could prevent them from installing the precious frog. However, the barricade was not strong enough to withstand the power of a charging locomotive. Angry Pennsy officials ordered another engine into action. With a fearsome charge, it plowed through the melange of rails, ties, tools and assorted debris before coming to an unseemly halt in the mud. This round went to the Pennsy, but the war was far from over, thanks to residents of nearby communities who sided with the smaller Delaware and Bound Brook.

By dawn the next day a throng headed for the Hopewell frog and, within hours, a mob estimated at more than 1,000 was milling around the tracks. The Governor sent the state militia to the scene as state officials mulled legal action to end the hostilities. Two days after the original Pennsylvania engine was rushed in to blockade the frog installation, the Governor ruled in favor of the Delaware and Bound Brook Railroad. The frog would be installed and the line could continue to Bound Brook.

The LIRR ultimately made Jamaica the heart of its system. This photo depicts Jamaica Station in 1870 before it reached its apex.
— Stan Fischler Collection

CHAPTER 5: COMMUTING IN THE 19th CENTURY — ONLY FOR THE HARDY

Long before the Civil War erupted, residents of New Jersey, Westchester and Long Island perceived the advantages of working in Manhattan while living in the country (suburbs). Railroad men knew this too, and as early as January 1838 the Morris and Essex line promised three-hour service between Morristown, New Jersey, and New York. A train enroute to New York left Morristown early in the morning and brought the intrepid businessmen back early in the evening. Conveniences of a sort were provided. In Morristown, for example, a bell tolled in the station *for a full hour* prior to the train's departure. This innovation came about after a trauma suffered by Newark commuters who had barely missed a New York-bound train scheduled to depart at 3:15 p.m. The "late" commuters had used the Newark town clock, which had registered at 3 o'clock, as their guide. The only trouble was that the Newark clock *remained* permanently set at 3 o'clock, since it had not been repaired for months! The commuters demanded that some more reliable form of pre-train warning be sounded and that is how the one-hour bell-ringing system evolved in Morristown.

Errant clocks, in time, proved less of a threat to the 19th century commuter than the physical hazards of the train rides themselves. Any time a rider boarded a Morris and Essex coach in pre-Civil War New Jersey, he was chancing an adventure which might take on any number of ramifications. For example, there was always a question as to whether the train would remain on the tracks. The Morris and Essex roadbed, in several places, consisted of two long logs laid lengthwise with timbers fastened crosswise. The "tracks" consisted of strips of bar iron attached to the long logs. It was not unusual for those lengths of rail to loosen. The engineer ("driver") and his co-workers, well aware of this hazard, carried a sledgehammer and spikes as part of their regular equipment to fasten loose rails.

An additional hazard developed when undetected rails, loosened further as the train rolled over them, occasionally pierced the undercarriage of a coach and threatened passengers with an unexpected bayonetting.

After a couple of round-trips a commuter could determine whether he possessed the courage and — more important — the patience required for train travel, for the stops made for "necessities" during early railroading were endless.

If the wood-burning engine ran short of fuel, the engineer would order his fireman ("wood-passer") to dismember a nearby wooden fence, load it on the train and toss it on the firebox. It was also *de rigueur* for the engineer to pull the train to a stop so that the crew could water down any trackside fire started by the spark-spewing locomotive. Invariably, the passengers' patience was further tried in Newark, where the cars were transferred from the Morris and Essex tracks, moved along Center Street by horses and then coupled to a New Jersey Rail Road and Transportation Company locomotive for the remainder of the journey to Jersey City.

Imagine the reaction of commuters on the Elizabethtown and Somerville when, in 1838, the engineer of the locomotive *Eagle* was challenged by a neighbor to a race. It was the classic confrontation between the iron horse and the race horse. The engineer couldn't refuse, and off they sprinted from Elizabethtown to Westfield, New Jersey, the hissing and moaning locomotive and the horseman pulled by a swift team of trotters. The horseman won the race handily, costing at least one commuter five dollars in lost bets.

Commuters on the Long Island Rail Road were confronted with a different kind of dilemma in those early days of steam. In one case residents vigorously demanded that the line *not* run trains — the milk run — on Sundays because fundamentalist Long Islanders considered it a violation of the Sabbath. Armed attacks against the LIRR protested the Sunday train. On August 12, 1858, a letter in the *Suffolk Times* charged that it would be "better that all men in New York and Brooklyn should drink water for one day, than the morals of the people should be destroyed." Anger against the Sunday trains reached such heat that the Long Island officials temporarily cancelled them. Once the critics had been pacified long enough, the Sunday trains were again dispatched.

During the administration of LIRR president Oliver Charlick, starting in 1863, trains were habitually late. Wrecks also were common.

In the hamlet of Quogue one Sunday, residents awakened to discover that the Long Island Rail Road *had taken their station away*. The unexpected move occurred as a result of controversy between villagers and the railroad over the precise location of the depot. Since the tiny station was built by Quogue residents, they believed that the station should be exactly where they put it. The railroad wanted it elsewhere. The LIRR high command made it clear that at the earliest opportunity, they would take the tiny depot and get it the heck out of there. A village historian described the ensuing events:

"The Quogue people kept a close watch on their 'station' (i.e. a shed) every weekday, and if the authorities attempted any dirty work at the crossroads on Sunday, the villagers would have them arrested for Sabbath breaking. But the boss of the LIRR was a smart Irishman named Cunningham and the authorities felt that they could leave the matter in his hands. So one Saturday night he brought a train crew to Patchogue, laid there all night and early in the Sabbath dawn they came the rest of the way; and the 'station' was 'moved' (dumped in the woods several miles to the east) before the Quogue people had awakened from their slumbers, as a means of reducing the obdurate people to a proper state of penitence and submission."

Disputes over station locations pockmarked the Charlick years. Inevitably, the commuters suffered. In the case of a spur to Syosset, Charlick and townspeople from Cold Spring collided over the depot site. In a fit of pique the LIRR boss simply killed the route, which had already been built from Syosset, and moved the track south of the town to spite the protestors. As a further humiliation to potential passengers who lived in the area, Charlick banned his engineers from even stopping south of Cold Spring! This public-be-damned attitude also was directed at Huntington, following a dispute between Charlick and a Huntington promoter. Charlick again switched routes and swung his track away from the original site (Huntington) to another (Huntington station) two miles away.

Northport was another community to feel Charlick's wrath and, to this day, commuters suffer as a result. In Northport's case, the community station was moved more than a mile south of the village. Contemporary passengers from Northport have to travel to East Northport for rail service.

Charlick was not the only tormentor of the early commuter. On the other side of the Hudson River, New Jersey train riders discovered that the men who operated their lines for profit were concerned only with profit — the rider be damned.

Long before the Civil War, passengers discovered the hard way — often at the expense of lives — that safety was neither a primary nor a secondary concern of the train barons, especially on the Erie Railroad. So synonymous did the Erie become with accidents that a Paterson (New Jersey) newspaper ran a headline in 1852 proclaiming: "A COLLISION! WE'RE GETTING USED TO THEM NOW!" Jersey City was forced to enact a law forbidding engineers to run trains at more than six miles per hour within the city limits.

Several moves made by the Erie seemed calculated to invite the undertakers. An early blunder was the railroad's decision to have its tracks spaced six feet wide instead of the traditional four feet ten inches wide. All was well with Erie trains when they rode on their own six-foot tracks but, too often, the Erie had to run its trains on the narrower tracks of other lines, such as the New Jersey Rail Road at Marion just west of Bergen Hill. The disasters occurred when switch tenders would mis-guess which train was coming and thereby upset a train or two.

One of the worst of the early Erie mishaps developed on the night of May 21, 1853, near Bergen Cut — an eastbound Erie express plowed into a westbound train engine-to-engine on the single track. Miraculously, no passengers perished, but the wreck cost two trainmen their lives.

Such collisions inspired some Erie employees to improve their lot. One progressive-thinking individual who tried was Pappy Ayres, a conductor on the Erie. He conceived the then revolutionary idea that the conductor — not the engineer — was in the best position to determine the condition of the train and when it should stop or start. Pappy's idea was to attach a rope to a stick of wood which would be located in the cab of the locomotive. By bouncing the stick, Ayres could notify the engineer when to stop and when to start. Not bargaining for the egomania of his engineer, Pappy installed his conductor-to-cab device and advised his engineer how he expected it to work. The engineer, unimpressed, discarded the stick with contempt.

Undaunted, Ayres replaced the stick with another and, once more, the engineer expressed his disdain by tossing it onto the tracks. The 300-pound Ayres was patient. He waited until the train reached its next stop and then marched up to the engineer's cab and boxed his colleague's ears. The engineer got the message this time and allowed the stick to remain. In time it evolved into a bell-and-pulley arrangement, later modified so that an air signal cord would notify the engineer.

Another Erie safety innovation involved the use of telegraph in controlling the run of the train. It was a terrific improvement for its time, but still left much room for collisions, especially in the era before installation of block signals. The major problem in the pre-block signal period of railroading was the method of stopping trains. A wire would be sent if a train did not pass a station when it should. The potential for disaster materialized when there was (a) man failure, such as a sleeping telegrapher; (b) failure of the telegraph machine; (c) the misreading of a message by the operator.

The first to address himself practically to a solution was Ashbel Welch of Lambertville, New Jersey, vice-president and engineer of the Camben and Amboy. Welch's theory was that no train should enter a *block* (a designated mile of track) until notified that it was clear, rather than proceeding until or unless a red light was shown.

"Welch's system was simplicity in itself," commented Joseph T. Cunningham. "It consisted of a box set on a post, with a white surface showing (a white light at night). As soon as a train passed a signal station a red flannel banner was dropped across the white surface (or white light) and it remained in place until telegraphed word was received that the block ahead was clear."

Unfortunately, the Welch block signal was not yet working on the Camden and Amboy on

March 7, 1865. Union Army troop trains regularly used the tracks between Philadelphia and Trenton. On that day two such trains, heading east from Philadelphia to New York, collided, one ploughing into the rear of the other. Six were killed and 40 injured in the wreck. It was almost another decade before Welch's system of block signalling was installed between New York and Philadelphia on the Pennsylvania Railroad main line.

Only a few railroad lords had the health and safety of their employees and passengers at heart. One such man was C.A. Wortendyke, president of the New York, Susquehanna and Western Railroad. When one of Wortendyke's trains collapsed a bridge in Saddle River, New Jersey, the line's president was so appalled that he personally devised a plan to test all of the Susquehanna's spans — firsthand. Wortendyke and several of his board members loaded themselves on a Susquehanna locomotive, which then was run out on all of the company's bridges. Then a second engine was run right behind the lead locomitve on the bridge to determine if there was a weak spot.

Wortendyke went a step further in the case of the Weasel Bridge, which spanned the Passaic (New Jersey) River. There he not only ordered two locomotives onto the bridge but also two cars filled with gravel, as well as workers, a number of newspapermen and company officials. Although the bridge proved its strength, the meticulous Wortendyke nevertheless mandated that it be bolstered even more against sagging.

Another line which took pride in its safety consciousness, albeit in a perverse manner, was the Lackawanna. Rather than indulge itself in such sophisticated devices as the Welch block signal, the Lackawanna boasted that its success would be maintained by "sober, capable engineers." And over a period of 40 years the Lackawanna suffered not a single passenger death. That record was tragically broken when a fog forced the Dover (New Jersey) express to decelerate near the Hackensack River drawbridge on a January morning in 1894. Coming up fast behind it was the South Orange (New Jersey) Accommodation. The engineer of the second train perceived the Dover express too late and rammed into the rear of it, killing 11 and injuring 35. Shortly thereafter the heavily-travelled commuter line began installing Hall-type automatic block signals, rather than relying on the sobriety and reflexes of its engineers.

By the latter half of the 19th century the number of improvements in railroading seemed to override the problems of corrupt or careless management. George Westinghouse's air brake, although poorly received at first, was a major breakthrough in speeding schedules while enhancing safety. Likewise, the automatic coupler, invented by Eli Hamilton Janney, gradually replaced the antideluvian link-and-pin couplers.

There was, sadly, one area in which the commuter railroads remained relatively impotent and that was in their handling of winter storms. In the late 1880's there were virtually no rotary snowplows in operation along the rails of the northeastern United States. Ironically, these efficient plows were already being manufactured in New Jersey, but they were sold, for the most part, to western railroads for use in the Rockies and other snowstorm centers.

The lesson that rotary snowplows were a local necessity was hammered home on Monday, March 12, 1888.

Nobody was thinking much about snow or plows on Sunday, March 11th. It was overcast, with a fine drizzle just bothersome enough to get under one's skin. But no bother. Work would not come until the morrow, and a good day of rest was welcome through the suburbs of New Jersey, Westchester, Connecticut and Long Island. The only portent of trouble was provided by the weatherman — assuming that the commuter of 1888 paid any mind to him — who reported that Monday's weather would be "clearing and colder." This turned out to be the forecasting understatement of the half-century.

As commuters across the metropolitan area tucked themselves into bed on Sunday night, the beginnings of The Blizzard of '88 were evident. The weather had turned sharply colder, snow was falling and winds were blowing harder and harder. By midnight, railroad executives on all the major commuter roads realized that their trains were in for trouble. Curiously, none took any significant steps to help the situation.

On Monday morning commuters discovered what a fix they were in —assuming anyone was brazen enough to challenge the blizzard. Yet railroad records indicate that an unusually large number of riders did trudge through the snowdrifts to their local railroad station. Perhaps they underestimated the intensity of the blizzard. Many no doubt assumed that, since it was almost the middle of March, the blizzard season was over. Others were motivated by the need to run their businesses in Manhattan, while still others placed an inordinate amount of faith in their local commuter lines. As one commuter put it: "No reason to worry, Mother, the good old Erie (or Jersey Central or Pennsylvania or Lackawanna) will be running. Nothing stops the Lehigh Valley. The Susquehanna always gets through."

Except they weren't getting through.

By 8 a.m. stations at every one of the commuter lines were filled with cold, anxious business people hoping somehow to reach New York City. When it became apparent to riders that the Lackawanna was losing its battle against the blizzard, some of them thought that if they could reach Newark the Pennsylvania would get them to New York. Frustrated riders of the Pennsylvania meanwhile shared the same thoughts about the Lackawanna. Snow continued to fall.

Of the major commuter lines the one that fared best in the early going was the Jersey Central, because the snows had not drifted over the plains south of the Watchung Mountains, along the Central's tracks. That explains why not one, but two Jersey Central trains chugged their way into Jersey City. The first of the pair arrived before dawn and the second, which had the more difficult time of it, pulled into the Hudson River terminal at 9:30 a.m. One newspaper reported of the second train:

"The train was crowded to its utmost holding. Snow and sleet came through the smallest crevices. It was not more comfortable than a refrigerator."

Those who made it to Jersey City had to question their luck, for now they had to take the ferry across the Hudson to Manhattan. On this morning the river currents were vicious, and a northeast gale was blowing so heavily that it was almost impossible for the captain to get the boat out into the river — but he did. A voyage that should have taken no more than ten minutes stretched into a half-hour as the captain battled his overcrowded ferry through the storm and ice floes. When at last he nosed the craft into its Manhattan dock, a chorus of cheers arose from the grateful passengers.

Meanwhile, the snow continued to fall.

By late morning it was evident that the Jersey Central was unique among the commuter lines. Hardly any of the others fulfilled their passenger-carrying obligations on this day and many experienced mishaps of the worst kind. To their credit, many railroaders made a doughty attempt to power their way through the ever-growing drifts, but the obstacles were too formidable. Lackawanna officials cringed when they received the news that no less than a dozen of their trains were stalled in the Oranges of New Jersey. Another pair of Lackawanna trains (from Montclair) stalled at Roseville, and locomotives that attempted to push their way through Bergen Cut were derailed. The closest Hoboken-bound Lackawanna train got stuck in snowdrifts in the Jersey Meadowlands.

The Lackawanna also attempted to move trains in a westerly direction. Three of them made it to an area between Brick Church and Orange, New Jersey, where they became mired. The engineer desperately used the last steam in his locomotive to summon help. Eventually the passengers slogged through the drifts on to the streets of Orange.

Depending upon the character of the passengers and their location in the blizzard, rescue operations took an assortment of forms. In the Meadowlands, one group of commuters took up a collection, raised funds and dispatched an expeditionary force to Harrison, New Jersey, where they obtained groceries.

Jersey City welcomed the more fortunate travellers who reached its assorted terminals. One group of vaudevillians, from a revue called "Dizzy Blondes," was treated royally by the Erie, which opened up its sleeping cars and allowed the troupe's female performers to make themselves comfortable for the duration of the storm.

Meanwhile, it kept snowing.

The Pennsylvania Railroad did a bit better than most of its rail colleagues. The line kept the westbound track open through Bergen Cut and was able to dispatch some trains from Newark to New York. According to one passenger, the train "writhed and snorted like a giant through the drifts."

When the snow finally stopped falling on Tuesday at noon, more than 50 locomotives had been derailed! It was now time to dig out, but the problem was how? The thermometer had dipped near zero Fahrenheit and Monday's snow had become Tuesday's ice. Locomotives froze in their tracks and more than 15,000 workers were sent out to get the trains rolling again.

Of equal importance was the job of administering first aid to the injured. In some cases help, unfortunately, arrived too late. At Musky Bridge, New Jersey, engineer Charles Baker was crushed to death under his locomotive, *Montclair*, which had been ordered to battle the drifts. At Flemington, two engineers and a fireman were killed in a derailment. In Jersey City a fireman on the Pennsylvania suffered a fractured skull when his engine jumped the track and rammed into a telegraph pole.

It was the Pennsylvania which recorded the first big breakthrough after the snow had stopped. At 5:20 on Tuesday afternoon the Pennsy ran a train through from Jersey City to Newark. The trip required three-and-a-half hours, but from then on it ran back and forth every 45 minutes through the night.

Other lines were less fortunate. The Lackawanna required two more days to restore complete service and the Jersey Central couldn't run trains to Plainfield until Wednesday night. The Erie ran trains to Paterson on Wednesday and welcomed its Chicago Express at Jersey City on Friday. It was only four hours late. Further calamity befell the Erie when a mass of rock fell from the roof of the Bergen Tunnel, closing the tracks once more. Luckily no trains were running through at the time.

By Thursday it was apparent that the army of shovel-toters was gaining in the battle against the snow. Frozen locomotives were warmed into action — kerosene-soaked waste was ignited under the carriages to melt the ice — and water was hosed back into the boilers. By Friday service was almost normal.

A week after the first morning of the blizzard, commuters debated the handling of the storm by their various railroads. It was generally agreed that the major error was the failure of any of the lines to employ the excellent rotary snowplow manufactured in Paterson, New Jersey. However, once the snow had melted, orders for the plows went out en masse. They passed their tests nobly, especially in November 1898, when another blizzard crippled the Northeast. Drifts of up to 15 feet blocked many sections of the Long Island Rail Road, but the LIRR handled the storm so well that none of its commuter trains were more than a half-hour late.

The LIRR commuter of the 1980's should be so lucky.

The LIRR operated two shuttles on many of its routes. This one linked Sag Harbor and Greenport. The photo was made at Bridgehampton in 1896. — Stan Fischler Collection

A Long Island Rail Road camelback locomotive awaits the strolling engineer.
— Stan Fischler Collection

CHAPTER 6:
ABOUT LOCOMOTIVES AND PASSENGER CARS

In September 1979 a story in *The New York Times* bemoaned the fact that the commuter railroads serving New York City were afflicted with inferior equipment and antiquated rolling stock. It was a story that could, with variations, have been written 150 years earlier, for the comfort of the passenger was not a primary consideration of railroad builders in and around New York in the first half of the 19th century. Pioneering passenger cars were simply glorified stagecoaches, the wheels of which had been adapted for riding on rails. Like the stagecoach, the early passenger car featured seats both on the inside and out. An outside seat was cheaper because the rider not only chanced inclement weather but also the possibility of being ignited by sparks which flew from the locomotive.

Thanks to a onetime horse dealer named Ross Winans (originally from Sussex County, New Jersey), the stagecoach-type car soon gave way to a passenger vehicle more closely resembling the rolling stock we know today. Winans, who ultimately became the designer of cars and engines for the Baltimore and Ohio Railroad, produced a more democratic and expansive passenger coach in the 1830's. All riders were confined to a long single inside compartment with seats flanking a middle aisle. Instead of riding on four wheels, the Winans car sat atop eight, which were housed in two sets of four-wheel trucks. Unlike the wheels on the stagecoach-type cars, the wheels on the Winan coach were also able to swivel, a major advance in the 1830's.

Interiors of the early commuter trains were spartan, to say the least. The seats, as a rule, were stiff-backed, accommodating two and sometimes three passengers in one seat grouping. Window space was plentiful. When the cold and snows came, two stoves — one placed at each end of the truck — provided too much heat for those unfortunates seated near them and too little heat for passengers located in the middle of the car. Riders unlucky enough to be seated away from the warmth of the stove could obtain temporary relief at station stops from peddlers who roamed the trains selling hot bricks to passengers.

The early locomotives were no bargain either. The *DeWitt Clinton*, built at the West Point Foundry in New York City for the Mohawk and Hudson Railroad, weighed a mere three-and-a-half tons and sported four iron driving wheels, but lacked a bell, whistle, pilot wheels, headlight, brakes or a cab. The engineer, like passengers sitting atop the coaches, was at the mercy of the weather.

The state of the art of locomotive-building was as basic as coach construction. For example, Matthias William Baldwin, an important pioneer in locomotive construction, had considerable difficulty with his first product. On its test run, Baldwin's engine attained a top speed of one mile per hour, and that with a good deal of pushing. But Baldwin persevered and soon perfected his locomotive so that it was able to reach a top speed of 28 miles per hour.

Baldwin, as well as many of his competitors, eventually settled into a design that, by mid-century, became known as the "American"-type locomotive. It featured two small wheels on each side up front — a four-wheeled truck — and four driving wheels (two on each side). According to

Oliver Jensen, author of *Railroads in America*, the American design was eminently suitable for its time. "The American embodied all the discoveries of twenty years, among them the leading pivoted truck, necessary for following the curving and lightly-built American railroads, and the 'four-coupled' arrangement of drivers invented in 1836 by Henry R. Campbell, which linked the four wheels that did the pulling into a single unit. It made the 'single', that is, single-axle, two-wheel engine, obsolete in America, although that design continued to be popular in passenger service on the fine, level rails in England, often with giant wheels as high as eight or nine feet! . . . The American style struck a rough, efficient balance; it would handle both, and take grades once thought impossible."

Several inventors, not the least of whom was Philadelphian Joseph Harrison, Jr., contributed improvements in the basic design. In 1838 Harrison, in an attempt to eliminate the slippage of driving wheels, developed an equalizing lever, which allowed the wheels on each side of the engine to revolve while resting their entire weight at a center point. "With an equalizer on each side," wrote Jensen, "and the flexible forward truck weighing on its single pivot, he succeeded in setting the whole locomotive on three points, in the manner of a three-legged stool, which will stand firm on an uneven surface, just as a rigid chair will not."

Nobody did more for the art of locomotive-building than Thomas Rogers. A native of Connecticut, Rogers moved to Paterson, New Jersey, in 1812. There he found work as a carpenter. "He made wonderful power looms," noted John T. Cunningham, writing of Rogers in the *Newark Evening News*, "and he turned out any kind of machine on demand." Rogers did so well for himself that he retired at age 39 with a reported bankroll of $40,000. This was in 1831, when the Paterson and Hudson River Railroad was being conceived.

Before Rogers could settle in his easy chair, he was approached by entrepeneurs Morris Ketchum and Joseph Grosvenor, who hoped to exploit Rogers' mechanical talent. Their aim was to do business with the Paterson and Hudson River Railroad. Interested, Rogers renounced his retirement and the trio, united under the banner of Rogers, Ketchum and Grosvenor, began coining money by making the ironwork for the new railroad's bridges over the Passaic and Hackensack rivers. This done, the burgeoning firm then was asked to assemble the railroad's maiden locomotive, obtained from Great Britain.

Rogers, who figured he could build a steam engine as well as he could assemble a night table, examined each part of the new locomotive with an Argus eye. Once the locomotive was assembled, Rogers rushed back to the drawing board and began designing his own engine. His efforts would ultimately result in the creation of the immense American Locomotive Company (Alco), to this day regarded as a titan of the industry.

Speed was not as important to Rogers as precision. He labored for 16 months before his engine, the *Sandusky*, was ready for the road. On October 3, 1837, the first locomotive produced exclusively by Rogers made its debut, although it had yet to be purchased. It was decided to give it a trial run on the Paterson and Hudson River tracks and, if all went well, to seek a buyer.

All went so well that J.H. James, president of the Mad River and Lake Erie Railroad, immediately put in a bid for the locomotive. Rogers accepted and a locomotive industry was launched at Paterson. Rogers' engine proved captivating right from the start. The *Sandusky* startled onlookers with a shrill blast that marked the first use of a railway whistle, ever.

The Ohio State Legislature was so impressed by the train that it required all railroads to use the same gauge as the *Sandusky*. And the commuter lines of New Jersey were soon ready to make purchases. The second locomotive to roll out of the Rogers, Ketchum and Grosvenor factory was delivered to the New Jersey Railroad. Again there was instant acclaim, and it was evident that Rogers, Ketchum and Grosvenor soon would have to re-tool for a major expansion. In 1838 three more locomotives were produced. By 1850 the expanded factory had upped production to 100 engines a year and was growing fast.

The future of Rogers' locomotive enterprise was guaranteed by one essential feature —

Suburban passenger (4-4-0) Engine #45, an American type, was built for the Long Island Railroad by Rogers Locomotive Works, Paterson, N.J., in 1888. Although small in size, these locomotives were capable of sustained speeds of 80 miles per hour. In 1895, Engine #45, along with several "sister" engines, was rebuilt by Baldwin into a Class D-53 camelback, serving in short haul commuter service until World War I, when most of them were retired because of the LIRR's electrification. — Stan Fischler Collection

quality. As one railroad critic noted, "Throughout the railroad world the talk was of Rogers and his locomotives. He tried everything — setting the wheels ahead and setting them back, experimenting with driving wheel diameters to increase speed or power. He tried hollow spokes; his counterbalanced wheels won him undying technical fame.

"Yet, powerful and durable though Rogers' locomotives were, it was their style — their pure class — that was foremost."

Rogers was also a trend setter, in that he had a passion for the beautiful product. The locomotives were lavishly appointed in a variety of colors. Yellow, red and blue paint adorned not only the wheels but the boilers and cabs. Bells, whistles, and other brass parts gleamed with polish.

Not that the Rogers, Ketchum and Grosvenor locomotive was without its detractors. Some critics charged that the engines, as a rule, swayed too freely. To that, Rogers countered, "I build locomotives to fit the road. They say my locomotives are wobbly. That's the way I want them to be. I put the body loosely on the wheels so the body can move around a little on the curves."

Rogers' standard of excellence rubbed off on his employees. In 1845 two of his better workers, William Swinburne and Samuel Smith, took their leave and opened their own factory, Swinburne, Smith and Company. In 1852 the name was changed to the New Jersey Locomotive Company and business boomed as it had for Rogers.

Still another Paterson, New Jersey, locomotive company appeared, Danforth, Cooke and Company, operating under the baton of Charles Danforth and John Cooke, the latter having been superintendent of Rogers, Ketchum and Grosvenor. Rogers attempted to keep Cooke on his payroll, but Danforth offered him a full partnership. Rogers gracefully accepted the inevitable.

Although Rogers' locomotives retained their superlative qualities, the railroad business grew so rapidly that there was ample room for Danforth also. At the time of Thomas Rogers' death in 1856, Danforth, Cooke; Rogers, Ketchum and Grosvenor; and the Grant Locomotive Works (formerly the New Jersey Locomotive Company) all were manufacturing engines in Paterson, which by 1860 had become the locomotive capital of the world. During the Civil War at least one locomotive was produced every working day at one of Paterson's three plants. Rogers was considered unexcelled in quality; Grant and Danforth were only a short step behind. As of the end of the 1881 business year Paterson could boast a grand total of 5,871 locomotives built there, all within an area of ten blocks, covering 645,000 square feet of factory space.

But in 1885 Grant moved its operations to Chicago. Then in 1902 Cooke was bought out by the American Locomotive Company, and in 1904 the Rogers plant was permanently shuttered. But even in the declining years the Paterson group attracted positive attention. Danforth and Cooke's rotary snowplow became a standard piece of operating equipment on all self-respecting railroads. A Rogers' triumph in a competition with a highly regarded British outfit (R and N Hawthorne) in the mountains of Chile led to orders from other foreign roads. "Even after the plant had been demolished," wrote Cunningham, "orders came in from foreign countries which refused to believe Rogers was no more."

Camelback locomotives of the D-53 class, were the mainstay of the Long Island Rail Road's engine fleet at the turn of the century and this engine, a rebuilt Rogers and Cooke 1890-vintage type, is shown emerging from the LIRR's Morris Park shops in Queens on April 24, 1899. The engine, and its sister-engines, was used in short haul commuter service in Queens and Nassau Counties up until electrification just prior to World War I. The cabs for crewmen were placed astride the huge boilers and the space allotted to crew members was so small that they were separated from each other, one on each side of the boiler. These coal burning engines were nicknamed "Mother Hubbards," and at one time the Long Island Rail Road had 53 camelback locomotives of four different wheel arrangements on its roster.

– photo courtesy of Long Island-Sunrise Trail Chapter, National Railway Historical Society

It was not uncommon for LIRR workers to line up for a portrait photographer. – LIRR

SECTION II — INTO THE 20TH CENTURY

CHAPTER 7: THE BIG SWITCH — FROM STEAM TO ELECTRICITY

As the first commuter railroads suffered growing pains early in the 19th century, a diverse group of inventors labored over the development of practical applications of electricity. Although no one realized it at the time, the efforts of such as English physicist Michael Faraday and American professor Joseph Henry would inalterably change the entire style of commuter travel. Faraday's contributions began in 1821 with the discovery of electromagnetic rotation. A decade later Faraday's experimentation revealed that electricity could be produced from magnetic force. Henry, meanwhile, worked on development of a practical electromagnet for an experimental motor that used magnetic attraction and repulsion to produce reciprocating motion.

Utilizing the knowledge gleaned from Henry and Faraday, a Vermont blacksmith named Thomas Davenport built a rotary electric motor for use on a small, circular electric railway. Unfortunately, Davenport's invention was too crude for immediate popular use. However, in Aberdeen, Scotland, Robert Davidson constructed a five-ton electric locomotive powered by a 40-cell, zinc-iron, sulphuric acid battery and electromagnetic motors. It was tried on the Edinburgh and Glasgow Railway tracks in 1838 and reached a top speed of four miles per hour.

Now the race was on for a workable electric train. Professor Moses G. Farmer developed an experimental locomotive in 1847 and ran it in Dover, New Hampshire. Then Professor Farmer collaborated with one Thomas Hall on a small electric railway that was put on public display at a fair in Boston in 1851. In the nation's capital Dr. Charles G. Page, an examiner in the United States Patent Office, produced a small electric locomotive, which on April 29, 1851, reached an impressive speed of 19 miles per hour while plying the rails between Bladensburg, Maryland, and Washington, D.C. Page was funded by a $20,000 grant from Congress. But the early electric trains still lacked commercial appeal. They all depended on the limited power of batteries.

In 1873 it was discovered that an electric motor could be made to generate electricity if rotated by mechanical means. In 1879 Dr. Werner Siemens constructed a short electric railway line at the Berlin (Germany) Industrial Exposition. Dr. Siemens' exhibit was a hit of the show. He pursued his project further and constructed another in Lichterfelde, and then a longer line between Portrush and Bushmills in Northern Ireland. Dr. Siemens' vehicle proved to be the first successful generator-powered electric train. Just a year later America's own Thomas Edison built an electric railway at Menlo Park, New Jersey. In effect, his experiment was too good for its own good. As John Anderson Miller observed in *Fares, Please!*, ". . . the locomotive ran so fast the passengers were nearly scared out of their wits."

A more ambitious electric railway project was suggested to Edison by Henry Villard, president of the Northern Pacific Railway. Villard felt that more than 40 miles of Northern Pacific track ultimately could be electrified if Edison's electric locomotive worked. In 1882 two of them — the vehicles had the appearance of small steam locomotives — were put on the track at Menlo Park. Unfortunately, financial woes riddled the Northern Pacific, and when Villard resigned, the project died. Nevertheless, the advances made by Edison and Stephen D. Field were united in 1883 under the banner of the Electric Railway Company of the United States. The firm displayed an experimental locomotive, *The Judge*, at the Chicago Railway Exposition. Obtaining its juice from a center third rail, *The Judge* carried 26,000 passengers at a speed of 12 miles per hour on a 1,500-foot, three-foot-gauge circular track. Subsequently, the electric train was installed at the Louisville Exposition, and it served as the prototype for an electric locomotive tried experimentally on the 34th Street elevated line in Manhattan.

Other advances in electrification were made, but nobody contributed more than a young United States Navy officer stationed in London in 1882. Frank J. Sprague frequently rode on the dingy, smoky Metropolitan District (London) underground railway, which operated steam locomotives. Sprague found the ride consummately distasteful, what with the soot and smell generated by the engines. It was a problem which, to a lesser degree, plagued New York's commuter railroads that passed through tunnels.

One day Sprague learned that a passenger on London's underground railway had died a few hours after taking a ride. A coroner's jury asserted that death, while due to natural causes, had been "accelerated by the suffocating atmosphere of the railway."

Sprague considered quitting the Navy on the spot to address the London problem. Instead, he waited a year and then formally resigned, whereupon he took a job as a technical assistant to Edison. In 1884 Sprague left Edison's firm and opened his own business, the Sprague Electric Railway and Motor Company. While he did not immediately address himself to the London situation, Sprague did take on an ambitious project for the Union Passenger Railway of Richmond, Virginia, for which he was asked to provide a power plant, a complete system of current supply and cars with motors. These cars were to be run on hills as well as curves, so that a true test could be obtained. Sprague was able to get the trolleys to conquer Richmond's steep Franklin Street hill. This first major street railway electrification won acclaim up and down the Eastern seaboard.

Meanwhile, Londoners finally got moving on electrification of lines previously earmarked for steam operation. In the 1880's Londoners watched with awe as construction work for the City and South London Railway progressed. Consisting of two tubes, each with a ten-and-one-half-foot diameter and running for a distance of three miles, the line ran from Stockwell to King William Street. John Anderson Miller described the ambitious project in *Fares, Please!*

"A shaft was sunk to a depth of 82 feet near London Bridge and boring started obliquely under the River Thames. Progress was made at the rate of about 80 feet a week . . . Construction was finished by June 1887, but the operation of the line did not begin until three years later."

The delay was significant. Originally, the City and South London Railway was to be operated by cable, but the startling advances in the field of electrification demanded a reappraisal. The technical press provided a catalyst by running innumerable articles about the advantages of electric traction. In August 1888 experiments with the electric traction reached a peak when C.E. Spagnoletti, one of the outstanding signal engineers of the era, was signed as a consultant of electric traction. Contracts soon were let and an experimental electric train was run through the tubes in December 1889.

The electric railway formally opened on November 4, 1890, the first electrically operated subway in the world. The occasion was considered of such moment that the Prince of Wales presided at the ceremonies. The City and South London Railway's electric locomotive was specially painted in cream and grey and named *Prince of Wales* for the occasion. On that same day the London Board of Trade granted the line permission to operate, and the first electric tube railway went into revenue service.

London's premiere electric route employed 14 locomotives built by Mather and Platt at their Salford Iron Works to the design of Dr. Edward Hopkinson. "Each of the axles," noted John R. Day, "was driven by a 50 horsepower motor with its armature built directly on the axles, the first time this arrangement, obviating gearing, had been used . . . The locomotives had air brakes but no air pumps, relying on large reservoirs which were recharged at Stockwell on each trip. There was no 'dead man's handle' in those days to ensure that power was cut off and brakes were applied if anything happened to the driver, so an assistant had to be carried on the locomotive."

The London electric locomotives pulled three passenger coaches seating 32 — two long seats facing each other across the car. The coaches were bereft of windows — slits near the roof were provided for ventilation — on the theory that windows were unnecessary in the subway since there was no light.

"These cars," wrote Day, "quickly earned the name of 'padded cells' — perhaps the company thought passengers needed them, because it also thought it necessary to forbid passengers to ride on the roof of the train! One car of each train was set aside for smokers, and ladies were forbidden to enter it. Each car had four electric lamps, but they were only of 16 candlepower each and not very efficient. They were always short of current, a situation which also made it necessary for the stations to be provided with gas instead of electric lamps."

Whatever its shortcomings, the London electric underground railways worked and, by the last decade of the 19th century, electric locomotives had proved that they were the match of steam engines.

Many of the major advances in electric traction took place in the United States, but not before a number of painful experiments went for naught. David G. Weems, a former associate of Frank J. Sprague, put together a two-mile test track at Laurel, Maryland, on which his electrified train reached a speed of 115 miles per hour. Additionally, he perceptively equipped his train with magnetic brakes, regenerative braking, streamlining and all-steel passenger cars. Oscar T. Crosby, whom Weems signed to conduct the tests, was responsible for many of the innovations, but the project never reached fruition because of lack of finances.

Like Weems and Crosby, Henry Villard had experienced financial failure with the Northern Pacific in 1884. But two years later, Villard merged Edison's electrical companies and the Sprague Electric Railway and Motor Company into the Edison General Electric Company in 1889, with himself at the helm. Then he turned his attention to a suburban commuter line, the Wisconsin Central, linked financially with the Northern Pacific.

Villard's idea was to electrify the railroad's Chicago terminal. To do so he hired Frank Sprague and Doctors Louis Duncan and Cary T. Hutchinson of John Hopkins University. The trio came up with a 60-ton eight-wheel locomotive built by the renowned Baldwin Locomotive Works. Completed in 1893, it was the largest electric locomotive to date, with a big steeple cab and enormous lanterns. However, the ill-starred Villard lost another bout with the banks. The Northern Pacific entered bankruptcy again before the locomotive ever took to the tracks. Villard got the hook as board chairman and all tests for the 60-ton engine were cancelled.

Although the failures were disillusioning, there were enough successes to assure that the electric way of travelling would work in the 20th century. The first took place in 1893 at Louisville, Kentucky, where the Kentucky and Indiana Bridge Company operated a five-mile steam railroad between Louisville and New Albany, Indiana. On August 25, 1893, the steam locomotives were shunted aside and replaced by oversized streetcars utilizing overhead wires. Electric cars continued rolling over the railroad bridge until 1945.

That same year the new General Electric Company plunged headlong into the electric locomotive business with a four-wheel 30-ton engine built at its factory in Lynn, Massachussets. At the World's Columbian Exposition, it was touted as "the first practically operated high speed electric locomotive in the world adapted to the requirements of the steam railroad." GE's second engine was purchased by the Taftville Cotton Mill in Taftville, Connecticut. It remained operational until 1964. GE had executed a giant stride in a field which would become intensely competitive by the turn of the century. It was at that time that one of GE's most formidable foes, the Westinghouse Electric and Manufacturing Company came into being.

GE's jump on Westinghouse was nullified in 1895 when the latter company obtained a contract to electrify the Burlington and Mount Holly (New Jersey) Traction Railroad Company. Although it was only a seven-mile branch line, the Burlington and Mount Holly offered Westinghouse the potential for big business since the spur was affiliated with the Pennsylvania Railroad. A trial run was held on June 3, 1895, with the lead car — resembling an interurban trolley, replete with overhead pole — pulling a traditional Pennsylvania coach. The electric locomotive was able to attain a speed of 60 miles per hour. Within two months of the experiment regular electric service was inaugurated on the Mount Holly line.

Westinghouse got its foot in the Pennsylvania Railroad door; General Electric did likewise with another fast-growing railroad, the New York, New Haven and Hartford. GE was encouraged by Charles P. Clark, president of the line, who was ready to electrify as soon as sufficient experiments had proven that it was more practical to use electricity than steam.

"If," said Clark, "electricity as a motive power becomes commercially practicable, the two interior tracks of the four now in the process of construction between New York and New Haven with their improved grades and alignment and absolute freedom from grade crossings will prove especially adapted to its use."

Clark approved an experiment on a small branch in Massachusetts called the Nantasket Beach line. The test, in 1895, proved so successful that Clark decided to electrify as many lines as possible on the New York, New Haven.

By now the cumulative results of the various electric experiments were so positive that the transit world was prepared for a major breakthrough in commuter railroad development. It would, as events would have it, take place rather appropriately on both the New York and New Jersey sides of the Hudson River, where the whole business of American railroading had begun.

CHAPTER 8: — THE HUDSON TUBES

Ever since the first commuter lines snaked across New Jersey, the railroads, out of necessity, established eastern terminals on the Jersey side of the Hudson River. The hope, of course, was that ultimately someone would devise a means of crossing the Hudson so that the trains could run to their most logical terminus — Manhattan.

Until a bridge or tunnel could be built, passengers enroute to New York City were compelled to get off at either Jersey City or Hoboken, among other "last stops," and then take a scenic — but often long and bothersome — ferry ride. By the latter half of the 19th century the river was heavily trafficked by trans-Hudson ferries.

The ferries were efficient in their own way, whether sidewheelers or the screw propeller type introduced by the Delaware, Lackawanna and Western Railroad in October 1888. But the challenge of speeding trains under the river loomed greater and greater.

One man, a colonel who fought with the Union Army in the Civil War, DeWitt Clinton Haskin, was determined to translate the dream of a Hudson River tunnel into reality. He based his optimism on the precedent of successful construction of a Missouri River bridge, in which a compressed-air-and-caisson method was employed to erect the span's piers.

Brian J. Cudahy in his book *Rails Under the Mighty Hudson* recalls the technology employed: "The technique involved a large inverted 'box' — or caisson — which was positioned at the site of the pier. The masonry pier itself was constructed atop the caisson, which began to sink into the river bottom. Compressed air was fed into the chamber to keep watery slime beneath the open bottom of the caisson out of the interior. Here workmen toiled, under pressure, excavating the downward journey of the caisson, a journey which continued until bedrock, or some other solid material, was reached."

Haskin figured that if the Missouri construction was expanded on a grand scale an underwater tunnel could, in fact, be burrowed from New York to New Jersey. He estimated that $10,000,000 would be needed for the project and organized the Hudson Tunnel Railroad Company. The precedent provided by the Missouri River construction proved attractive. Armed with sufficient funds to launch the project, Haskin watched with glee as construction began in November 1874 from the Jersey side of the river.

In time more than 1,000 feet of brick-lined tunnel was constructed under the Hudson but, unfortunately, that was as far as the Haskin tunnel could go. Constructing vertically was not a problem — nor was it at the Missouri River site — but the horizontal aspect of the digging proved extraordinarily slow and terribly hazardous. Disaster occurred on July 21, 1880, when 20 sandhogs were drowned in a blowout. The number might have been higher were it not for the heroism of Peter Woodland, a sandhog trapped in the airlock when the blowout began. As his colleagues raced for the pressurized door which supposedly would lead to safety, Woodland perceived that the loss of pressure in the tube would engulf even those who believed they had reached a safe spot. Woodland chose to close the door of the airlock, thereby eliminating any chance he or 19 others in the airlock with him had for survival, but his valor enabled the others to clamber out of danger.

The blowout was merely one of innumerable problems which bedeviled the project after its enthusiastic beginning. Haskin's money ran out; he began losing his sight; and an endless series of injunctions, coupled with financial reverses and accidents such as the 1880 calamity, finally brought the project to a halt.

But other promoters stepped forward to prove that an under-the-Hudson tunnel was a feasible engineering proposal. Less than a decade after the tragic blowout, the British-backed Hudson River Tunnel Company took over where Haskin had left off and burrowed an additional 1,600 feet toward Manhattan. By 1890 there was reason to believe that the company supplying the know-how — S. Pearson and Sons, the outfit which built the much-acclaimed Forth Bridge in Scotland — would successfully push the tunnel through to New York.

One asset that Pearson possessed and Haskin had lacked was an advanced underwater boring mechanism called "The Greathead Shield," named after English engineer Sir James Henry Greathead, which eliminated potential blowouts while accelerating burrowing at the river bottom. Armed with the shield and an abundant amount of optimism, the Hudson River Tunnel Company not only proceeded toward the Manhattan shore but also initiated work on a second tube to be built alongside the first.

Alas, just when Pearson's army of laborers appeared on the verge of completing the first tube to Manhattan, another spate of difficulties — not the least of which was fiscal — caused construction to grind to a halt. Skeptics began to wonder if the tunnel would ever be completed. As fate would have it the entrepeneurial requirements necessary for the task were supplied by a Southerner named William Gibbs McAdoo, who left a law practice in Chattanooga, Tennessee, to make a name for himself in New York.

In some ways McAdoo seemed an unlikely choice to orchestrate the grand Hudson River underwater project. A native of Dixie, he was not privy to New York or New Jersey political machinations, nor was he as intimately familiar with railroading or tunnel-building as some of the engineers and trainmen who had expressed interest in the tubes. But McAdoo adapted well and with a keen business mind went searching for information about tunnelling under the Hudson. In 1901 McAdoo, along with prominent New York engineer Charles M. Jacobs, gingerly trod the muddy innards of the Hudson tunnel.

McAdoo later wrote; "The fates had marked a day when I was to go under the riverbed and encounter this piece of dripping darkness, and it would rise from its grave and walk by my side. I was destined to give it color and movement and warmth, but it would change the course of my life and lead me into a new career."

McAdoo and Jacobs were trying to determine whether anything was salvagable from the works of Haskin and Pearson. McAdoo was relying on Jacobs' expertise. When Jacobs, who had masterminded the first subaqueous tunnel in New York under the East River in 1894, reported that the existing tunnel was utilizable as far as it went, that was good enough for McAdoo.

It was now four years since Frank J. Sprague had developed the multiple-unit control system for rapid transit (which permitted two or more units of electrical equipment to be operated from one control point). Thanks to this discovery McAdoo believed that the Hudson tunnel project could be exploited into a rapid transit money-maker. Rather than utilizing steam-powered locomotives, Haskin's potentially dangerous plan, McAdoo conceived an all-electric commuter line, not unlike the Interborough Rapid Transit (IRT) subway then being blueprinted for the bowels of Manhattan.

Taken to its furthest limits, McAdoo's trans-Hudson commuter subway would link not merely the Jersey shore with Manhattan, but also would have an assortment of tentacles throughout New Jersey, including a main line run to the metropolis of Newark.

McAdoo soon obtained the necessary financial support, and for the third time an attempt was made to link New York and New Jersey under the river. "Construction was no easy task," observed Brian Cudahy. "Rock ledge was frequently encountered even in the deepest portions of the river

MAP OF THE TUNNEL SYSTEMS

of New York and New Jersey, showing connections with and stations of the great McAdoo system known as

The Hudson & Manhattan Railroad Company

The north tubes of the system, under the river, are each 5700 ft. long, 15 ft. 3 in. in diameter, constructed of steel rings cemented and bolted together, and concreted on the inside. Work was done by: Haskins Co., 1874—80; Haskins Co. (No. 2), 1890—92; N. Y. & Jersey Co., 1902, and completed by them in 1905. Second tube constructed by reorganized N. Y. & Jersey Co., as The Hudson and Manhattan Railroad Company, 1908. Opened to the public, Tuesday, Feb. 25, 1908.

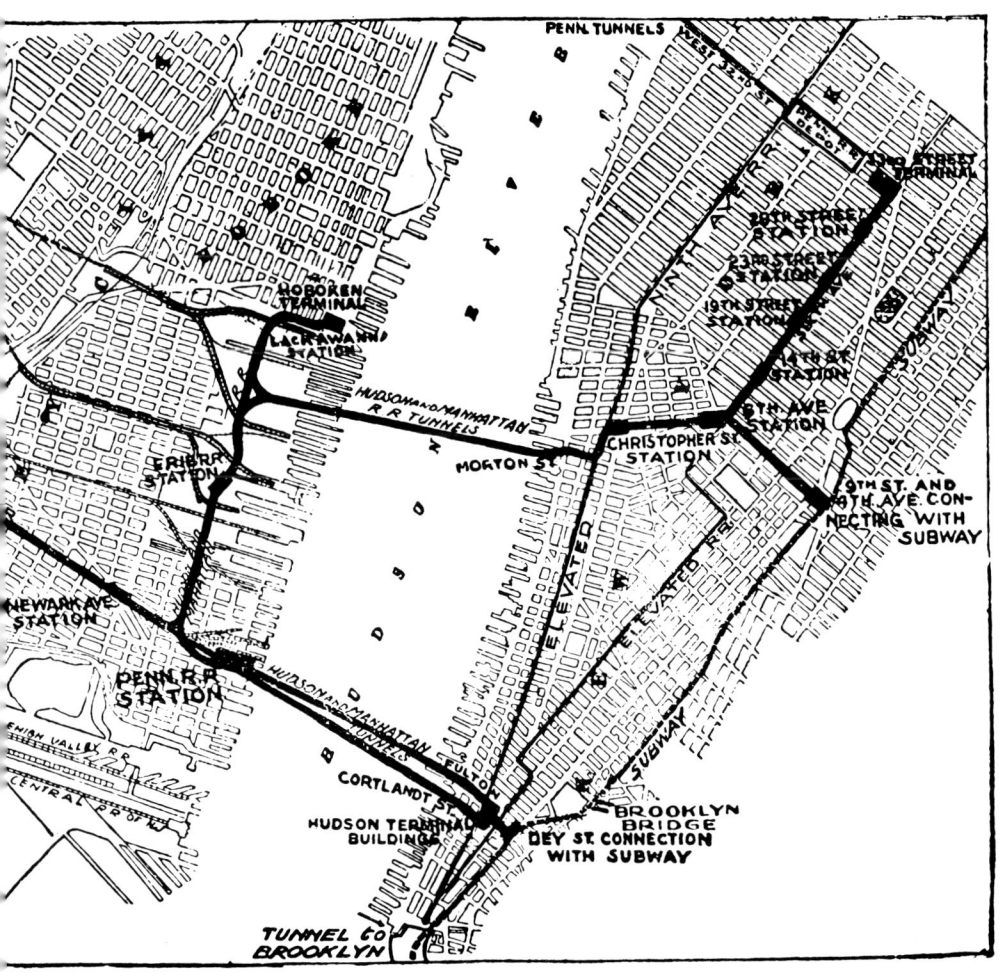

bottom. At one time engineers were faced with the devastating prospect of a formation of reef rock that rose up twelve feet from the bottom of one of the tubes, a tube whose outside diameter was eighteen feet. In other words, while blasting was necessary at the bottom of the tunnel, the top had to be pushed forward through soft mud silt at the same time."

McAdoo chose wisely when he named Jacobs his chief engineer. A number of successful innovations were introduced during construction, not the least of which was the baking of watery silt over the shield into hard clay by means of hot torches brought into the tunnel.

Working from the New Jersey side, Jacobs' sandhogs burrowed toward the New York shore, the target a tunnel originally begun by the Pearson group. Exactly 404 days after work had begun, the linkage was accomplished.

In anticipation of the triumph, Jacobs had rigged a temporary telephone from the tunnel to McAdoo's office. When the final burrowing was completed the chief engineer invited his boss down for a look-see. When McAdoo arrived, Jacobs took him in hand and they clambered through a door in the shield. From there they explored the 5,650-foot tube from end to end, an experience which later moved McAdoo to exult, "For the first time in the history of mankind, men had walked on land from New Jersey to New York."

McAdoo next invited a horde of journalists. To the surprise of some who had earlier expressed open skepticism, the trip was completed without catastrophe. They realized that there would be no holding back completion of the comprehensive Hudson and Manhattan Railroad. Construction already was underway on the Manhattan spur of the H and M. It would link the downtown (New York) terminus at Christopher Street in Greenwich Village with a new station at East 19th Street and Sixth Avenue. Across the river the line was stretched north to the Hoboken terminal of the Delaware, Lackawanna and Western Railroad.

The vigorous McAdoo pushed forward construction of a second pair of trans-Hudson tunnels even before the first pair had been completed. Rather than connecting with Greenwich Village, the newer tunnel would speed the electric trains to a new station to be located at the base of a skyscraper called Hudson Terminal, within shouting distance of New York's City Hall. Equally ambitious were plans for the Jersey side of the new tunnel. Couplings would be made with the Pennsylvania Railroad's Exchange Place station, with the sizeable terminal of the Erie Railroad, and there would be a connection with the Hudson and Manhattan's own pair of tubes — the originals — at Hoboken.

While all this was going on workmen forged ahead, completing the original tunnel in preparation for the operation of the new trains. Meanwhile, an elaborate bill of particulars was established for the selection of rolling stock for the H and M's first fleet of trains. McAdoo hired the respected consultant, L.B. Stillwell, to head the group writing specifications for the cars. When completed, the blueprints recommended that the cars be relatively lightweight, fireproof and permit rapid exit and egress.

The finished product was an advanced design for its day. Built simultaneously by the American Car and Foundry Company and the Pressed Steel Car Company, the cars were 48 feet long, eight-and-a-half feet wide and weighed 64,000 pounds. Each car offered a set of three doors on each side — one at each end and one in the middle — and smartly arranged windows. In the railway industry, McAdoo's rolling stock was rated above that already in use on New York's widely-heralded IRT subway.

In December 1907 the line began running cars filled with sandbags instead of passengers through the Hudson tunnels. Within a month the time had come to test the trains with people instead of sandbags. D-Day was set for January 15, 1908. On that day, McAdoo led an entourage down the stairs to the station at Sixth Avenue and 14th Street, where an eight-car, freshly-painted steel train awaited them. When all dignitaries had taken their seats the company's superintendent, E.M. Hedley, pulled the heavy steel controller handle in the motorman's cab and the train rolled slowly toward the tunnel, easily negotiating the curves that eventually brought it to the straight-

Construction of the underwater link between New York and New Jersey was a courageous and difficult task as these photos indicate.
— Stan Fischler Collection

Prior to the opening of the new tubes, the spanking new "McAdoo cars" were stored on an outdoor siding.
— Stan Fischler Collection

A commemorative medal heralding the grand event.
— Stan Fischler Collection

William Gibbs McAdoo (second from right) conducted an inspection of construction of the Hudson & Manhattan Tunnels beneath the Hudson River on September 29, 1905.
— Port Authority of NY and NJ

On the inaugural run, the motorman and company officials pose in mid-tunnel for a portrait. — Stan Fischler Collection

away and the dip down under the Hudson. The excursion reached Hoboken without mishap and then returned to Manhattan, where McAdoo was toasted as the man who had mastered the underwater crossing of the Hudson River.

The Hudson Tubes were opened to the riding public on February 25, 1908. McAdoo, eventually to become Secretary of Treasury under President Woodrow Wilson, pulled out all stops for the Tubes' world premiere.

A telegraph machine was installed on the platform of the H and M station at Sixth Avenue and West 19th Street, with connections to the White House in Washington, D.C., where Theodore Roosevelt was presiding as chief executive. According to plan, the juice through the third rails would be shut off on signal, whereupon a telegrapher would transmit a message to President Roosevelt: "The first official train of the Hudson and Manhattan Railway Company under the Hudson River awaits your signal and your pleasure. W.G. McAdoo."

When the message was received at the White House, Roosevelt pressed a button on his desk which, in turn, dispatched a signal to the H and M's substation, where power was then thrown "on" for the Tubes' third rail. Next the motorman pulled on the controller and the train moved toward the tunnel, still redolent of fresh concrete. At the front window were the governors of New York and New Jersey, Charles Evans Hughes and Franklin Fort. Like the other dignitaries aboard the inaugural special, the governors were particularly concerned that the new commuter line fulfill its promise of high-speed transit to and from New Jersey. As it turned out, the ride consumed ten-and-a-half minutes, which would be the normal running time once the line began actual revenue service.

Interest in the inaugural ride was so high among Manhattan's elite financial community that the H and M's planners could not find enough room on the eight-car consist for all who wished to ride under the Hudson. As a result, a ninth car was called and still many notables were forced to stand.

Cornelius Vanderbilt III, grandson of the famed Commodore Vanderbilt, was one of the standees; he seemed untroubled by the inconvenience. No less enthused were the good burghers of Hoboken, who welcomed this high-speed link with the Gotham. A crowd estimated at 20,000 filled the streets around the new H and M terminal in Hoboken, where toasts were delivered to the Tubes. Beaming from ear to ear, the prideful McAdoo was handed a congratulatory message from President Roosevelt, which he read to the audience.

Eventually, McAdoo led the party back into the arch-ceilinged Hoboken Terminal, where they boarded the train for the return trip to Manhattan and a commemorative dinner at the swank restaurant, Sherry's. Meanwhile, the riding public — less interested in the fuss and fanfare generated by millionaires — eagerly awaited its chance to plunk down some coins and buy a ticket for the Tubes. The honor of being the first passenger to purchase a ticket on the new Hudson and Manhattan line belonged to a Mrs. Barbara Schlatter of Hoboken, who was among the throng which had lined up early in the bitterly cold evening for the privilege of being Number One on the H and M.

When the first New York-to-Hoboken train arrived, a pair of straphangers named John Gladner and Richard Scully indulged in a spontaneous race to the train, prefiguring a sprint many thousands would soon make to catch a connecting train.

If completion of the tunnels was a triumph for McAdoo so, too, was construction of the vast Hudson Terminal in downtown Manhattan. It was here that the boss of the H and M demonstrated his meticulous concern for perfection. One day he appeared at the construction site as steeplejacks prepared to hoist a huge steel girder to the top of the skyscraper. To the utter astonishment of the steeplejacks, McAdoo said he would like to ride on the girder as it was pulled. And that is precisely what he did, standing like a sure-footed Indian as the steel was lifted to its lofty position.

McAdoo had many plans for his line; most were realized, but not all of them. He had hoped to operate the Tubes northward in Manhattan under Sixth Avenue to 42nd Street and then curve east, where the H and M would connect with Grand Central Terminal. But the Tubes never made it past 33rd Street, a point reached in 1910.

On the plus side was the extension of service in 1911 over the Pennsylvania's tracks to Newark. That same year the very practical and rather interesting Manhattan Transfer station opened near the Passaic River on the H and M line to Newark. It was at Manhattan Transfer that the Pennsy's huge steam passenger locomotives subsequently ended their eastbound runs to be replaced by enormously successful side-rod-drive electric locomotives. The machines — known in the trade as DD1's — hooked up with the passenger train as soon as the steam locomotive was removed. In no time at all the train was off again, enroute to its terminus at Pennsylvania Station at Eighth Avenue and 33rd Street in Manhattan. For those Pennsy passengers who preferred making Lower Manhattan their destination, there was a Hudson and Manhattan train sitting at an adjoining platform ready to deliver riders to Hudson Terminal.

The Newark connection not only meant more flexibility for the Tubes' service, but also resulted in improved rolling stock. The original H and M rolling stock — known as "Black Cars" — featured a lightly curved roof and stylized twin windows. When service was extended to Newark the H and M, in conjunction with the Pennsylvania Railroad, bought a fleet of more highly-powered cars from the Pressed Steel Car Company and designated them MP-38's.

Painted Tuscan Red, rather than H and M black, the new cars featured a flat roof and highly distinctive porthole windows in the front. Like all the Hudson Tubes rolling stock, the MP-38's took their power from the lines' steam generating plant in Jersey City. This unit had two 6,000-kilowatt and two 3,000-kilowatt Curtis turbines. Power was distributed at 11,000 volts A.C. to substations, where it was converted to 600 volts D.C. for the Hudson and Manhattan's third-rail system.

Once the Newark run was established, the Hudson Tubes became a commuter line to reckon with, not merely because of its speed, its scope and its flexibility — tying in with major

The Sixth Avenue station at Herald Square dominates this early 20th century Manhattan scene with the Hudson Tubes kiosk on the lower right. — Stan Fischler Collection

Now out of service, the Tubes' 19th street station was the acme of artistry.
— Stan Fischler Collection

transcontinental rail lines — but also because of its philosophy. Straphangers from Greenwich Village to Newark appreciated McAdoo's "The Public Be Pleased" slogan as sincere. If the customer wasn't always right on the H and M, McAdoo made him feel as if he was right 99 percent of the time. It seemed as if the boss of the Tubes was determined that his railroad would outdo August Belmont's nearby IRT subway. McAdoo even went so far as to hustle business on incoming ocean liners and, of course, glorified the virtues of the Tubes in an extensive advertising campaign.

Few could argue with the results. The passenger ridership graph described a steady upward climb. As World War I flared in Europe, the H and M boasted an annual ridership of almost 60,000,000 passengers, with the best years yet to come. Apart from the Tubes' first-rate service there were other meaningful reasons for this happy event, not the least of which was the Manhattan Transfer.

The post-World War I era was a golden age of railroading and no line in the country did better than the Pennsy, which was all to the good as far as the H and M was concerned. By sharing platforms with the PRR at Manhattan Transfer, the Tubes couldn't help but fatten ridership figures. But what made Manhattan Transfer so utterly unique was its inaccessibility. There was no other means of reaching the station except by either Pennsylvania Railroad or Hudson Tubes. "Many stories are told," said Brian Cudahy, "of fortune hunters from places like Dubuque or Duluth who long nurtured the American Dream of 'hitting it big' in New York City. After days of traveling they were understandably misled when a conductor stuck his head inside the coach and announced 'Manhattan Transfer.' They presumed this station to be their long-sought destination, the promised land. The punch lines vary, but the stories turn on the station's complete and total lack of egress to city streets."

Manhattan Transfer, which handled more than 200,000,000 passengers in its lifetime, was immortalized by novelist John Dos Passos in a 1925 book of the same name. The station remained operational even after the Pennsy electrified its system west and began phasing out its steam locomotives. But when the big railroad opened its lavish new terminal in Newark in June 1937, all the transfers previously made at Manhattan Transfer could be more expeditiously made in Newark. Thus, on June 20, 1937, Manhattan Transfer was permanently shuttered.

Complementing the growth of the Tubes was the boring of several tunnels by the Pennsylvania Railroad and construction of massive Penn Station at Eighth Avenue and 33rd Street in Manhattan. One of the tunnels ran underneath the New Jersey Palisades as well as the Hudson River, thereby carrying the railroad's main line directly into midtown Manhattan. Still another PRR tunnel headed eastward from Penn Station under Manhattan and the East River to a site in Long Island City where a sprawling storage and repair yard was built. These projects were completed by 1910 and created a smooth yet subtle unity between the H and M, Pennsy and Long Island Rail Road, the latter of which utilized the tracks eastward from Penn Station and beyond the Sunnyside Yards in Long Island City.

Little changed in the structure of the Hudson Tubes through the post-World War I years and into the Roaring Twenties. By 1927 passenger ridership had reached an all-time high of 113,000,000, many of whom rode new cars acquired during the early 1920's. The last fleet of new cars, built by the American Car and Foundry Company, proved to be the last batch of new rolling stock to arrive for 30 years (until 1958). In the interval the Tubes had become as much a part of the woof and warp of New York life as the IRT, Penn Station or the Woolworth Building. The distinctly musty smell of the tunnels had an intoxicating effect on many. Hudson Terminal displayed a charm all its own, and McAdoo's inimitable "black cars" gave the Tubes a character that would remain through the World War II years. Unfortunately, the surge in ridership, which peaked in 1927, ended with a steady decline through the Great Depression decade.

As efficient as the H and M may have been, it was now confronted with formidable competition from automobiles using a network of tunnels (Holland, Lincoln), bridges (George Wash-

Interior and exterior view of an early Hudson Tubes car at Journal Square Station.
— Port Authority of NY and NJ

The streets of Greenwich Village are virtually empty at the Tubes' Christopher Street Station in this early 20th century view.
— Stan Fischler Collection

ington, Goethals) and highways crisscrossing the metropolitan area. Gasoline was still cheap and abundant.

In the early 1950's the Hudson Tubes plunged into bankruptcy. On the bright side, however, was its purchase in 1958 of 50 air-conditioned cars from the St. Louis Car Company. The rolling stock — 20 of which were owned by the Tubes and the others by the Pennsy — was a marvel of its time and eventually inspired the conservative New York City Transit Authority to add air-conditioned cars to its lines.

The cars were but a cosmetic cover-up for the fiscal problems which bedeviled the line. A solution of sorts was obtained in 1962 when the Port of New York Authority, one of the most powerful transportation organizations in the nation, agreed to purchase and operate the Tubes. After considerable legal hassling, the deal was consummated and the onetime Hudson and Manhattan Railway Company became known as the The Port Authority-Trans-Hudson Corporation, an operating subsidiary of the publicly owned Port Authority. Those with strong roots to the glorious past referred to the newly purchased old line as "The PATH Hudson Tubes," being unable to drop the name which had become so familiar to New York and New Jersey commuters.

Some transit critics were skeptical of the Port Authority, noting that the agency seemed dedicated to the encouragement of auto travel in the metropolitan area, but the facts proved otherwise, and in no time at all significant improvements took place.

The once magnificent Hudson Terminal was doomed by the Port Authority, which drew up blueprints for a twin-towered skyscraper to be known as the World Trade Center. Hudson Terminal, as a depot for the Tubes, was replaced by a new air-conditioned H and M station featuring longer platforms to accommodate an expected growth in ridership. Equally important was the placing of an order for 206 new air-conditioned cars from the St. Louis Car Company. These differed markedly from the 1958 models, in that they boasted a stainless steel covering and were lavishly appointed and streamlined to the nth degree.

Dissatisfied with the state of the Tubes' physical plant, PATH launched an intensive rehabilitation of the line, from signalling to electrical power distribution. The Port Authority acted wisely since, one by one, the Hudson River ferry boats began closing down. In November 1967 the last of the ferries — this one operated by the Erie Lackawanna Railroad — ended its Manhattan-to-Hoboken runs. The result of this spate of improvements was an encouraging growth in ridership. In 1972 an additional 46 cars were delivered to PATH by the Canadian-based Siddeley firm.

The upgrading of the H and M's plant and the infusion of smart, new rolling stock gave the Hudson Tubes a vitality that had been lacking since the McAdoo years. In fact there was a time, in the mid-1970's, when it appeared that another building program — though not on the grand scale of the early 20th century — would push the Tubes into new territory.

One blueprint would have the PATH line extend beyond Newark's Penn Station to Newark Airport, also operated by Port Authority. Another plan was to extend the Tubes to the suburb of Plainfield, New Jersey. So far, neither of these major extensions has been undertaken. At the moment of the 1980's the same basic configuration exists as when William Gibbs McAdoo imagined the line at the turn of the century.

CHAPTER 9: TUNNELS, A SUPER BRIDGE AND A MAMMOTH TERMINAL

At the turn of the century two titans of railroading, the Pennsylvania and New York Central, challenged one another for the leadership in passenger travel in the East. This healthy competition provided rich rewards for not only the long-distance traveller but for the commuter as well. Within the first two decades of the 20th century, for example, New York area commuters were treated to the construction of two genuinely awesome depots that did a land-office business in commuter ridership. Electricity replaced steam as the dominant form of propulsion, and a spate of other engineering marvels modernized rail travel far beyond the dreams of 19th century planners.

In the battle for customers the New York Central possessed one major advantage over the Pennsylvania Railroad: the Central had direct access to mid-Manhattan, whereas its rival pushed its rails only up to the Hudson River's west shore, from there a ferry carried riders into the city. There was additionally the advantage the Central had developed with its construction of Grand Central Terminal.

Tentative plans that the Pennsylvania nurtured for an extension into New York — by bridge or, even more daring, by tunnel — were dropped because of the financial panic of 1873. When the panic subsided in the early 1880's new moves were initiated. In 1884 plans were developed for a high-level bridge over the Hudson which would rise to 135 feet in the clear, with its Manhattan approach reaching a terminal near Desbrosses and Canal streets in the downtown portion of the city.

There were a number of immediate difficulties to overcome, such as the federal government's refusal to allow construction of bridge piers between the pierhead lines of the river because of congested harbor conditions. Despite this restriction, engineers still believed that a practical span could be erected, and plans were developed until another financial crisis — this time The Panic of 1884 — once again put them back on the shelf.

Less than a decade later another span was proposed to cross the river near 23rd Street, with a depot to be located near Sixth Avenue and 26th Street. This proposal seemed feasible, but depended on other railroads also using the span. When the Pennsy failed to induce other companies into the project, the scheme bit the dust.

Successful operation of the electrified Orleans Railway into Paris, France — switching from steam locomotives at Austerlitz — inspired Pennsy planners in 1901 to consider a possible model for a trans-Hudson project. A.J. Cassatt, the Pennsy's president, visited the Orleans Railway and returned to the United States enthusiastic. By this time the Pennsylvania had acquired controlling interest in the Long Island Rail Road, which meant that designers would be asked to come up with a terminal for both the Pennsy and LIRR, as well as a physical connection between them and an outlet to the New England states. The depot, of course, would be located somewhere in Manhattan. Thus, tunnelling would have to take place under both the Hudson and East rivers if a link with the Long Island lines was to be effected.

"You are requested," wrote Cassatt to his corps of engineers late in 1901, "to procure all additional information that may be needed, sparing neither time nor any necessary expense in doing so, for I am sure it is not necessary for me to say that, in view of the magnitude and great cost of the proposed construction, and of the novel engineering questions involved, your studies should be thorough and exhaustive, and should be based on absolute knowledge of the conditions."

Cassatt dubbed his engineering commission "The Board of Engineers" and set January 11, 1902, as the date of their first formal meeting. For business purposes two construction companies were incorporated, one in New York State and the other in New Jersey. Five years later, in 1907, they were merged under the banner of the Pennsylvania Tunnel and Terminal Railroad Company, a corporation of both states.

On December 23, 1902, New York City's Board of Aldermen passed a resolution approving a franchise for extending the railway under the Hudson River to a passenger station located in Manhattan and thence under the East River to a connection with the Long Island Rail Road.

Integrally linked with the Pennsy project was a spate of improvements on the Long Island Rail Road, including electrification of the commuter line within the city limits, construction of freight stations on the line from Bay Ridge, Brooklyn, to East New York and, most significantly, rejuvenation of the Atlantic Avenue Division, a bustling passenger carrier running at street level across Brooklyn. Homeowners along the route wanted the trains taken off the streets and put either in the air (on an elevated structure) or underground. The LIRR did both. It erected a handsome new terminal at Flatbush and Atlantic avenues in downtown Brooklyn in 1906 and constructed tunnels under Atlantic Avenue eastward to Bedford Avenue, where the tracks climbed out to the first "el" station at Nostrand Avenue. The elevated double-track then proceeded east above Atlantic Avenue until it re-entered a tunnel at Eastern Parkway and Atlantic Avenue.

Cassatt's Board of Engineers completed their plans and presented them for approval. Among the essential projects was an offshoot of the main line of the Pennsylvania Railroad near Newark. The new spur would cross the Hackensack Meadows, burrow through Bergen Hill and thence under the Hudson.

From the new station four tubes would tunnel under the East River, linking with the Long Island Rail Road in Queens and a new passenger train yard in Sunnyside, Queens. James Kip Finch, an engineering historian, described Cassatt's venture as "one of the boldest and most courageous undertakings ever conceived by the creative imagination of man."

Construction work began in 1904. From the public's viewpoint — since sidewalk superintendents could view the work — the most impressive project was development of the colossal Pennsylvania Station on eight acres of land bounded by 31st and 33rd streets and Seventh and Eighth avenues on the west side of Manhattan.

The distinguished architectural firm of McKim, Mead and White designed the depot. Designed in the Roman Doric style, the terminal, when completed in 1910, was the Pennsy's pride and joy.

Of all the aspects of the new Pennsylvania Station none was more awesome than the main waiting room, a huge vaulted hall considered a reasonable facsimile of the Baths of Caracalla in Rome. Upon its completion the waiting room was the largest of its kind in the world, with a floor area of more than 30,000 square feet and a ceiling 150 feet above street level.

In a commentary published by the Isaac H. Blanchard Company after Penn Station was completed, William Couper observed: "As we enter, the daring color treatment is at once apparent. The pleasing effect of the travertine, of which the interior is constructed and which has since the days of Roman ascendancy been a favorite building material abroad, pervades the atmosphere and adds a thrill which is tempered only by the silence — the awesome silence when we realize that there is no audible evidence of the hastening throngs seen all around us.

The original Pennsylvania Station is seen in all of its magnificence, looking southwest from 33rd Street. Note the incomplete steel work in the right background.

— Museum of the City of N.Y.

"The most salient feature of the station is the main waiting room; so large is it that many of the best known hostelries in the country could be placed in this one room. Spaced about the lofty travertine walls are enormous Corinthian columns, standing on pedestals, which support the coffered vaulted ceiling. At the north and south ends of the room there are colonnades of Ionic columns and immediately below the six large lunette windows which surround the room are panels on which have been painted conventionalised maps in colors blending with the beautiful, warm, sunny color of the travertine."

The coupling of the Pennsy and the Long Island Rail Road was a major plus for commuters. Planners of Penn Station went out of their way to cater to the growing commuter clientele, even when it came to providing toilet facilities. As Couper noted: "A boon to the commuter are the luxurious pay toilets. Luxurious, you say. Yes and why? Mr. Commuter has a dinner and theater engagement. In the good old days he had to engage a room at his club or a hotel, change his clothes there, return to the hotel at the end of the evening, secure his suitcase and then hustle to the station. Now he goes to the station, where in the morning he checked his suitcase, engages a so-called pay toilet, which in reality is a small room built of Carrara glass provided in addition to the usual toilet facilities with a wash-basin, towel, soap, whisk, mirror and chair. Here he changes his clothes, shaves if he wishes, and after rechecking his suitcases proceeds to keep his engagement. For a small coin he has fulfilled all requirements and saved a trip at a later hour in the evening."

Among other amenities provided for the passengers were an exclusive waiting room for the Long Island Rail Road patrons, a first-class restaurant, modern ventilation for summer and winter and, for the employees, a YMCA replete with gymnasium, lounge and library.

Construction of the station was completed in 87 months. At the time it ranked as the largest building in the world constructed at one time. The Vatican, the Tuileries and the St. Petersburg Winter Palace all could boast that they encompassed more area, but centuries were involved in the construction of all three edifices.

Opening day, November 26, 1910, was not without its irony. At 9:30 a.m. the depot opened for business and the first person to fork over his cash for a ticket was not the mayor, the president of the Pennsy or a Broadway star. Rather it was an anonymous commuter acknowledged by one newspaper as "a little man" who sped across the shiny, new terminal floor and bought himself a round-trip ticket to Elizabeth, New Jersey. "How anomalous," wrote Brian Cudahy in *Rails Under The Mighty Hudson*, "that a station which would become the gateway to the nation, that would dispatch through sleeping cars to Florida, California, Canada and Mexico, sold its first ticket for a ride into the nearby suburbs."

The first train to roll westward was not one of the Pennsy's great liners, such as *The Broadway Limited*, but rather a local for Perth Amboy, New Jersey.

If the Pennsy's high command suffered any doubts about the success of the new venture and its impact on New York City and its suburbs, the doubts were put to rest within weeks of opening day. The depot worked efficiently and provided land-office business to concerns tangential to the terminal. Street car lines in the vicinity were compelled to add more rolling stock to keep pace with the passengers feeding in to Penn Station, and merchants within blocks of the depot enjoyed a rise in receipts.

Unfortunately for metropolitan area commuters the city fathers of New York failed to keep pace with the Pennsy's progress. It was clear that the hordes of commuters travelling to and from the new terminal required a means of rapid transit which was not available to them in the 33rd Street area at the time. New York's first subway was already open when Penn Station began operating, but it ran up the east side of Manhattan and didn't curve west to Broadway until 42nd Street. Noted Pennsy vice-president Samuel Rea, ". . . while the company has not yet produced facilities for subway connections, the city has not yet produced these necessary rapid transit facilities to accomodate its own citizens and the public arriving and departing from the new station. It is a matter of deep regret that the city's subway system, with proper connections, is not complete or ready to perform their necessary function."

Nevertheless, the Pennsy did perform its necessary function with nobility. A fleet of new electric locomotives — the DD1's — speeded its riders through the tunnels to Manhattan Transfer in New Jersey, where the electrics were replaced by the railroad's long-range locomotives. It was a splendid arrangement with more improvements on the immediate horizon.

"Pennsylvania Station and its miles of tunnels under Manhattan and the rivers brought both Long Island and New Jersey into much closer communication," wrote Lawrence Grow in *On the 8:02*.

"A trip from the Newark area to the business centers of Queens and other eastern Long Island manufacturing towns was made feasible for the first time. In effect, the Pennsylvania Railroad substantially increased the extent of the operative range of the New York industrial market to both the east and west of Manhattan. All of this was accomplished long before automobile tunnels and bridges further enlarged the commercial circle.

"The Pennsylvania's tunnels brought the commuter to his place of work and home again much more rapidly than did the old ferry service. Pennsylvania Station was intelligently designed and positioned to make maximum use of connections with (what was to be) Manhattan's subway system."

Among the many features of the new operation about which the Pennsy could boast, none drew more comment than its superb new side-rod electric locomotives, otherwise known as the "remarkable DD1's." Although only two tracks were available to the train under the Hudson, the high-speed electric locomotives were capable of handling as many as 144 train movements per hour between Manhattan Transfer and Pennsylvania Station. The amazing electrics not only were efficient but durable — two DD1's continued in service until the early 1960's.

Completion of the Penn Station complex, the Long Island Rail Road connection and other facets of the linking of New Jersey, Manhattan and Queens went according to schedule. Expansion of the Hudson and Manhattan Railway (Hudson Tubes) and its link with the Pennsy further eased the life of the commuter, but there was still more work to be done: specifically, action on a plan originally proposed in 1892 to form a coupling between the New Haven Railroad, with all its New England business, and the Pennsylvania.

Early in the 1890's Pennsy official Samuel Rea had come up with an elaborate proposal to tie in the railroads of New England, principally the New Haven, with the Pennsy. A link of sorts was already in existence via a trans-Hudson bridge at Poughkeepsie operated by the New Haven line. Still another connection was in use, railway cars were ferried between the New Haven yard at Port Morris, New York, and the Pennsylvania freight depot in New Jersey on Upper New York Bay. It was an unsatisfactory 14-mile boat connection.

The New York Connecting Railroad was organized in 1892. The aim was to form the connection in New York, specifically by means of an East River bridge at Hell Gate. But the idea remained unrealized until the turn of the century, when the gala Pennsy expansion began taking shape. In 1902 the Pennsylvania and New Haven lines cooperatively bought the stock of the New York Connecting Rail Road. Now it was merely a matter of time before the bridge was built. Naturally, the Pennsy wanted a first-class span erected and, to this end, they hired Gustav Lindenthal to draw up the master plans.

Lindenthal already had an impressive track record as a bridge-builder and had come very close to designing a bridge which would have brought Pennsylvania trains into Manhattan over the Hudson rather than under it. However, the U.S. Army Corps of Engineers vetoed that plan with the result that the Hudson River tunnels were built instead. When Samuel Rea, already a Lindenthal booster, took command of the railroad in 1913 he hired him to orchestrate the Hell Gate project.

According to the blueprints, the connection between the two railroads would begin at the New Haven's Harlem River branch at 142nd Street in the Bronx, then curve across the Bronx Kill to Randall's Island, then the Little Hell Gate to Wards Island, then cross the Hell Gate. Ultimately, it would link with the vast passenger yards in Sunnyside and the Long Island Rail Road. From Sunnyside, the trains coming over Hell Gate would be able to roll under the East River to Penn Station.

Lindenthal undertook the project with great relish. Not only did he design what was to be one of the greatest bridges in the world, but he supervised the construction of it right down to the last bolt. Lindenthal, an Austrian immigrant, had come to America in 1874 and alternately worked as mason, bricklayer and draftsman. In time he was hired as an architect of a prominent company. It was an ascent consonant with his philosophy. "Failure," said Lindenthal, "is only an epitaph for a lack of preparation."

Preparation was basic to the success of Lindenthal's Hell Gate Bridge. At first a suspension bridge was thought more appropriate and practical. If not a suspension bridge, a cantilever span would do the job — and relatively inexpensively. But Lindenthal finally opted for an enormous arch-type span because he believed that it would form the most impressive gateway to the Long Island Sound entrance of New York harbor. Writing in *The Bridges of New York*, author Sharon Reier notes: "No existing large span bridge had ever been designed with such huge parts. Some of the steel members were more than twice as heavy and bulky as any parts ever hoisted in previous bridge construction . . . the bridge, it was said, used more steel than the Manhattan and Queensboro combined."

Lindenthal determined that a span of such enormity would have to sit on solid rock. This was not a problem on the Queens side, where such rock was discovered less than 40 feet beneath the surface. However, such was not the case at Wards Island, where the rock was irregular and much deeper than at the Queens end. Earlier a fissure had been found which, engineers concluded, could severely weaken the bridge's foundation. At this point the genius of Lindenthal and his associates came to the fore.

"The resourceful engineer decided the underground chasm could be bridged just as one on the surface could," wrote Reier. "He threw a concrete arch across the fissure where it passed through the center of one of his rectangular caissons. At another point where the fissure lay at a joint between two of the caissons, he bridged the gap by means of a concrete cantilever. The idea of building concrete bridges in a caisson was absolutey original and a contribution to engineering technology."

With the foundations in place, Lindenthal next turned his attention to the actual skeleton of the bridge. Since the waterway at the time was frequently used, Lindenthal could not use falsework — the normal process in erecting an arch bridge — in constructing the span. To compensate for the absence of falsework, Lindenthal decided to construct the bridge by "overhang" from each of the foundation piers until they ultimately united in the middle.

Another compensatory decision was to place the steelwork on huge temporary structures built onto the towers. A delicate counterweight operation had to be effected here to balance the weight of the incomplete parts of the arch. Again, Lindenthal proved the successful innovator. This type of operation had never been performed before.

"There is a spirit of adventure in every big bridge," said Lindenthal. "The careful engineer — and no other kind should be allowed to build a bridge — has every detail calculated, but there is the adventure of seeing the plans work out perfectly and the haunting dread that perhaps some detail will fail."

None did, as Lindenthal resorted to more massive equipage than was the norm in such construction. Special large rivets, heavy splicing, special pivots and breaking girders in the floor were among the innovations produced. The blueprint called for the arch to support four ballasted railroad tracks. As impressive as the mighty arch was to become, so, too, were the twin towers at each end of the span. One newsman wrote of the towers: "With the addition of a few hieroglyphs, the new concrete piers of the approaches to Hell Gate Bridge would be unmistakably Egyptian. They are 75 feet high, and as you look down through the archways, you think you are standing in the portico of a mammoth unfinished temple."

One of the most extraordinary bridge designs of any railroad in the world is the Hell Gate span over the East River in New York City. The Triborough suspension bridge looms in the background. – Museum of the City of N.Y.

Even in its unfinished state, the span compelled attention, but never more than on the day the two arms of the arch were scheduled to be linked at the center 280 feet above the water. So accurate was the engineering that when the steel was fitted in place the adjustment required to bring them into line was less than half an inch!

On the Queens side of the bridge an impressive steel-and-concrete elevated structure weaved its way to its confluence with the Pennsy. By 1916 the major work on the monumental span was completed. The longest steel arch bridge in the world — outdistancing its closest competitor by 200 feet — it also ranks as the strongest bridge of its kind.

Although only four locomotives were likely to be on the bridge at any one time, the structure, if necessary, could hold 60 locomotives, weighing 200 tons each, laid end to end. As it happened, when Hell Gate Bridge enjoyed its heaviest usage it never carried more than 70 trains each way daily.

The goliath project officially opened for business on April 1, 1917. Later that year the New York Connecting Railroad was joined to the Long Island Rail Road's Bay Ridge line. The coupling provided direct access between the New Haven and a new car-float terminal at Bay Ridge.

At first steam engines provided the only motive power over Hell Gate Bridge, but in 1918 electrification of the passenger line came about.

The opening of Hell Gate Bridge meant a complete change in the movement of passenger trains from the south and west into New England. From 1876 until the Hell Gate's debut through passenger cars from, say, Boston to Washington, were placed on a steamer which transferred them from the Pennsy yard at Jersey City to the New Haven's tracks at Mott Haven, the Bronx.

For all its splendor and utility, Hell Gate Bridge never quite fulfilled its commercial promise. Its opening was almost immediately followed by the onset of America's entry into World War I. Though traffic flourished to a certain extent, railway business began to decline.

What can not be denied the Hell Gate Bridge is the artistry of the engineering feat itself. It stands today, as impressive architecturally as ever, although somewhat tarnished because of pollution, benign neglect and the ubiquitous graffitti that characterize rapid transit facilities in New York City. Similarly, the Pennsy's tunnels are still operating as efficiently as ever but, alas, one cannot say the same for Penn Station.

The depot, considered a classic of its time, suffered the ultimate indignity in the early 1960's, when railroad passenger business had reached its nadir in this country. Commuter traffic continued flourishing on the Long Island Rail Road tracks into Penn Station, but the long-haul trains had fallen victim to the anti-railroad sentiment which, curiously, the passenger lines themselves had fostered. Magnificent Penn Station was doomed to rubble. Recession-plagued New York City was seeking ways and means of boosting its economy, its tax base and its ego. It also was a time when the management of the "old" Madison Square Garden on Eighth Avenue and 49th Street were casting about for a site on which to build a brand new sports and entertainment complex. The result was a decision to raze glorious Penn Station and replace it with a combination office building, refurbished railroad station and a brand new Madison Square Garden. Better still, the new Garden would be located atop both the Long Island Rail Road tracks, as well as the numerous city subway lines which by now converged on the Penn Station community.

Not surprisingly, the decision to erase Penn Station from the face of Manhattan was viewed with alarm, anger and incredulity by a healthy segment of New Yorkers. The *New York Times* indignantly editorialized against what it called "monumental vandalism." Nevertheless, in 1965 the wrecker's steel ball began crashing against the columns lining Seventh Avenue while railbirds watched with mixed emotions.

The Long Island Rail Road was able to continue commuter operations as usual, since the LIRR tracks and platforms all were situated underground and erection of the new structures took place above track level. There was amazingly little disruption of service, considering that 500 new support columns had to be sunk into bedrock without impeding the flow of trains.

Today, the former site of the great Pennsylvania Station is occupied by a bland, 29-story office building, adjoined by the circular "new" Madison Square Garden. There is no overt sign of a railway station, until one notices commuters dashing from the escalators to the assortment of LIRR tracks below.

Fortunately, the New York Central's railroad depot of Promethean proportions, Grand Central Terminal, remains alive and well.

CHAPTER 10: GRAND CENTRAL TERMINAL

From the beginning of commuter railroads in the New York metropolitan area, locations suitable for terminals to receive the various lines was a perplexing problem. The difficulty hinged on Manhattan's growth northward from its original Dutch settlement (New Amsterdam) at the southern tip of the island. The community could only grow in a northerly direction, which meant that the earliest railroads actually plied some city streets, to the dismay of the burghers.

Annoying as it was to many residents (and horses didn't care much for the steam engines either), the railroad was still enough of a phenomenon to elicit tolerance, until the city began bulging at its seams. By the end of the Civil War, time had come for a truly grandiose depot befitting the metropolis. Railroads were here to stay, and most of them regarded New York City as their logical eastern terminus, underlining the point that a vast structure was needed to embrace the many lines.

Heretofore, station-building had been a relatively shabby art in North America. Most lines concentrated their funds on such essentials as rolling stock, tunnels, bridges and track. Architectural experts such as Henry Hudson Holly, author of the first American pattern book to include plans for a railroad depot, deplored the state of the railroad station in the United States prior to the Civil War:

"In Britain," wrote Holly, "stations are beautiful and tasteful, just as their trains are safe and luxurious." By contrast, Holly noted, American stations were "uninviting or ridiculous, beggarly or pretentious."

There were exceptions, to be sure. The most outstanding of the early stations was designed by architect Henry Austin for the city of New Haven in 1848. It was described in *Benham's City Directory and Annual Advertiser* as "a beautiful edifice. "On either side of the main hall or platform are extensive parlors, that on the left side being for the accommodation of ladies and is furnished with a profusion of rich and costly sofas, divans, chairs, ottomans, mirrors, etc., with convenient dressing rooms attached. Obliging servants are always in attendance . . . The design of this beautiful structure . . . reflects the highest credit on the architect . . . Long may it stand as an enduring monument to the taste, the liberality and the enterprise of its projectors."

Oliver Jensen, in his *Railroads in America*, points out that even the handsome New Haven station betrayed several flaws. "The building," writes Jensen, "was at street level; trains ran through a cut, and passengers had to descent to narrow, smoky and inadequate platforms in order to board them.

"A small boy, getting off the cars into the steam and gloom, remembered his Calvinist upbringing and asked his father, 'Is this Hell?' 'No, my son,' replied his father, 'New Haven.'

While New Haven's railroad station was capturing the attention of designers around the country, the man who ultimately would build the biggest and best station for its time in America was making a mint in the steamboat industry, with no thoughts of railroading.

Commodore Cornelius Vanderbilt got his start at age 16 operating a produce and passenger-carrying sailboat across New York harbor. By the Civil War he had become a multi-millionaire, world-ranging shipper. Vanderbilt was a natural for the railroad business, but he repeatedly rebuffed suggestions that he invest some of his shipping wealth in steam engines. "Bring me a steamboat," countered Vanderbilt, "and I can do anything, but I won't have anything to do with your damn railroads!"

Somewhere along the line, however, the Commodore underwent a dramatic revision in his thinking. In 1863 Vanderbilt purchased the New York and Harlem Railroad. Few realized it at the time, but the 70-year-old Vanderbilt was on the threshold of building an empire which would dwarf his vast shipping interests.

One by one the Commodore added railroads to his portfolio. The New York and Harlem was followed a year later by the Hudson River Railroad and, in 1867, by the New York Central Railroad. The latter acquisition provided Vanderbilt with enough trackage and rolling stock to push his combined New York Central and Hudson River railroads — with a few notable additions — all the way from New York City to Chicago. Now it was time to select a site, hire architects and erect a palatial terminal to house his profusion of trains.

Where to locate this depot? That was the question. In the years immediately following the Civil War, the area north from the Battery to 23rd Street was relatively well-populated, but acreage as far north as 42nd Street, where the New York and Harlem Railroad steam locomotive facilities were located, was still regarded as God's country. Streets were still unpaved and residents of the city considered 42nd Street as far, far from the madding crowd: certainly no place to erect a comprehensive rail station. Yet that was precisely the location selected by the foresightful Commodore. "Everyone," wrote Oliver Jensen, "thought it was a great joke, building a station so far uptown. The newspapers christened it the 'End-of-the-World Station.'"

Forty-Second Street may have been a 45-minute horsecar ride from City Hall at the time, but Vanderbilt realized that the relentless population surge inevitably would move the city's center further and further north. Besides, there were other practical reasons for selecting 42nd Street as the depot site, not the least of which was a municipal ordinance forbidding steam engines south of 42nd Street.

The honor of designing the structure was bestowed upon Isaac C. Buckhout, Vanderbilt's trusty chief engineer for the Harlem Railroad. Buckhout and the Commodore's son, William H. (Billy) Vanderbilt, were the chief overseers of the project. By the end of 1869 all red tape had been cleared and on September 1, 1870, the initial foundation stone was set in place.

In every way, from scope of design to sheer physical immensity, the project was awesome. The train shed of the terminal, a gaping, cylindrical mouth of wrought-iron, rose 100 feet in the middle and 200 feet at track level. Running 600 feet in length, the shed was designed by engineer R.G. Hatfield and constructed by the Architectural Iron Works of New York, which also produced the elaborately detailed cast-iron girders. A total of 12 tracks were housed under the shed — patterned after St. Pancras Station in London — along with five platforms, each a step above track level. Two of the dozen tracks continued southward, through a pair of portals and down to the original station at Fourth Avenue and 27th Street.

No less impressive than the shed was the facade at the north end, from which the rolling stock emanated. Topped with huge lettering — "ERECTED 1871" — the facade comprised a curtain wall of glass and iron, and included a small cupola from which the railroad's dispatcher monitored the incoming and outgoing trains.

The 42nd Street, or southern, end of the station, which contained waiting room, ticket-selling and other necessary facilities, was designed by architect John B. Snook and, in many ways, was the most impressive aspect of the entire $3,000,000 project. The L-shaped edifice continued from 42nd Street around to Vanderbilt Avenue, which was created for the station. Author William D. Middleton in his book, *Grand Central: The World's Greatest Railway Station*, describes the terminal's Second Empire facade as "finished in rich, red pressed brick with ornamental coins, cornices, and window frames of cast iron, painted white in imitation of marble. Five ornate mansard-roofed towers surmounted the 42nd Street and Vanderbilt Avenue facades."

The original Grand Central Station on 42nd Street, in the pre-automobile era. Note the electric street car (left), as well as the horse car (center) plying the rails. The huge Hotel Manhattan looms in the background.
— Library of Congress

Commodore Vanderbilt's wisdom in building the depot at the 42nd Street location was borne out. The wide crosstown street soon was paved with cobblestones and, naturally, became the recipient of a new crosstown horsecar line.

Another seemingly vexing problem, which was quickly solved by the Commodore, involved a linkage between trackage heading north from the proposed depot and his Hudson River Railroad tracks, which heretofore continued along the western perimeter of Manhattan Island to St. John's Park and the line's freight house at Canal Street. What Vanderbilt needed was a linkage in northern Manhattan along Spuyten Duyvil and thence to the tracks which flowed along the east side of Manhattan down to 42nd Street. The Commodore unravelled the knotty problem with remarkable ease. He began in 1869 by forming the Spuyten Duyvil and Port Norris Railroad, which then laid seven miles of track from the Hudson River to the Harlem line's tracks at Mott Haven. From Mott Haven south to 42nd Street the three railroads utilized the Harlem's tracks into the city.

The vital linkage was completed in 1871 in time for the grand opening of Grand Central Depot, the official handle for Commodore Vanderbilt's opulent terminal. "It was a gaudy building," recalls author Oliver Jensen, "a cross between the Louvre and a cast-iron toy bank. Critics complained that it was wanton to slap a slate mansard roof onto a Renaissance building, but it is highly unlikely that the Commodore was disturbed by this sort of carping."

Why should Vanderbilt complain? He now was maestro of the foremost railway station in North America, one which served not one but three different lines — the New York Central and Hudson River, the Harlem and New Haven — and one which seemed imposing enough to last a century.

In fact, it wouldn't survive a half-century.

Grand Central Depot was obsolete the moment it opened, and this depressing fact was partly a function of the Commodore's vanity. When Vanderbilt inspected the two acres of glass on the station's roof he became appalled at the prospect of the elaborate glass becoming defaced by the soot belching forth from his steam engines. How, then, could the passenger cars be delivered and dispatched from the train shed?

"This meant some very tricky railroading," writes Jensen, "when the trains came in. The floor of the shed was tilted so that departing trains had only to release their brakes and coast out to where the engines were waiting; but arriving trains had to be 'switched on the fly.' As the train approached the station the engineer braked a little to give the brakeman some slack at the couplers. At a signal from the whistle the brakeman pulled the pin, uncoupling the train from the engine, which darted over to an adjacent track.

"The open switch swung shut behind the engine, and the cars coasted up into the station. This maneuver was every bit as dangerous as it sounds, yet we are told that there was never an accident."

Another problem: the 12 tracks into Grand Central Depot were hardly enough to meet the demands of the three railroads. This problem defied solution through the turn of the 20th century. Yet another vexing issue was smoke.

Right from the start smoke proved an annoyance to both Commodore Vanderbilt's passengers and New Yorkers who lived near the depot or plied the streets in the immediate vicinity of the train shed. The problem became aggravated in 1876 when an additional six terminal tracks were laid to accomodate the increase in traffic. By far the worst situation existed in the Park Avenue tunnel at the edge of the station. There, according to one report, "the smoke was frightful." There were a number of recorded incidents when engineers fainted from the coal gas. Accompanying firemen, to protect their lungs, stretched themselves along the bottom of the cab on the assumption that they could therefore avoid the worst of the smoke.

The black clouds gushing from the steam engines occasionally blotted out the engineer's view of the red and green signals near the terminal's entrance. This led to disaster in 1902. A commuter train operated by the New York, New Haven and Hartford Railroad was halted by a red signal. It was the morning rush-hour and another train, this one belonging to Vanderbilt's New York Central line, was approaching *on the same track.* Ordinarily it would have halted at its own red "Stop!" signal, but smoke had obscured the red light, and the New York Central express plowed into the rear of the commuter train. The disaster cost the lives of 17 passengers. It also inspired demands for the elimination of polluting steam engines in and about the depot area.

Grabbing hold of a good issue, New York's politicians developed a far-reaching law, ultimately approved by the State Legislature, forbidding steam locomotives from entering Manhattan after July 1, 1910, on passenger service. Fortunately, the Vanderbilt family had chosen well when it appointed lieutenants. In this case the job of revamping Grand Central to accomodate electrification fell on the shoulders of William J. Wilgus, the depot's chief engineer. Electrifying the station in itself would be a monumental project but, in addition, Wilgus realized that the station would have to be expanded considerably to accommodate the relentless growth in both commuter and long-distance railroading.

Electrification seemed, off-hand, like the easier of the two projects. After all, electricity had already proven its usefulness on Manhattan's elevated lines and soon would be utilized on the subway lines to be built under the city streets. But finding more room was a more perplexing dilemma, since Grand Central's 48 acres could not be added to by more than a few feet.

Over and over again Wilgus was confounded by restrictive geography — Vanderbilt and Lexington avenues on the west and east, 46th and 42nd streets on the north and south. It seemed a problem without a solution — until Wilgus had a brainstorm. Why not depart from the conventional single level of tracks and construct two levels; one for the commuter lines and the other for long-distance trains.

Although the idea was rather revolutionary it passed muster when presented to the board of directors. Now it was a matter of finding the right architectural firm to construct the new terminal. Because of the colossal nature of the project, a number of prestigious architectural firms immediately expressed interest in the assignment. New York-based architect Stanford White was among the favorites to win the nod. Also in the running: a Philadelphian with excellent credentials, one Samuel Huckel, Jr.

White, partner in the firm of McKim, Mead & White, formally entered the competiton with a blueprint calling for a station embellished by a 700-foot office tower, topped by a 300-foot illuminated jet of steam. Huckel's offering was a multi-turreted office building with adjoining hotel wings, sitting atop the terminal. Both plans were grandiose but consonant with the rapid development of mid-Manhattan and the city's obsession with skyscrapers.

Another entry was submitted by a firm in distant St. Paul, Minnesota, headed by Charles A. Reed and Allen H. Stem. Although they lacked the attention-grabbing qualities of a Stanford White, Reed and Stem had considerable experience in the design of railroad terminals, having done work for five different lines and no less than 90 stations. Reed and Stem had another advantage not commonly known at the time to most casual observers: New York Central's Wilgus was married to Charles Reed's sister.

Whether nepotism ultimately played a part in the eventual choice of architect is irrelevant in terms of the finished product. Reed and Stem produced a Grand Central blueprint that was consonant with Wilgus's vision. Of vital importance was the manner in which the architects arranged for the continuation of Park Avenue from the southern end of the terminal at 42nd Street through the northern side at 46th Street. Both Huckel and White planned to carry Park Avenue directly *through* their proposed buildings, whereas Reed and Stem produced an alternative which appealed to the railroad's executives. The Minnesotans suggested that Park Avenue be carried up a ramp south of 42nd Street and then be wrapped around the depot along elevated roadways, thus preserving the unity of its interior spaces.

The Reed and Stem design which won the competition was innovative in that, for the first time in American railroading, stairways were replaced in a major depot by wide, gently sloping ramps. However, not long after the St. Paul company began drawing up blueprints the New York Central hired another firm to assist in the architectural planning.

A New York company, Warren and Watmore, joined Reed and Stem. Though Whitney Warren, senior member of the Warren and Wetmore outfit, was a cousin of William K. Vanderbilt, the Commodore's grandson and then chairman of the board of the New York Central, Warren's eminence as an architect was such that nobody could rightly claim that he had been pulled in by a Vanderbilt's coattails.

While the architects convened over ways and means of designing the final version of the new terminal, Wilgus began orchestrating the razing of Commodore Vanderbilt's original Grand Central Depot. The trick, of course, was to tear down the old train shed while maintaining the precise scheduling of both the Central's and the New Haven's innumerable incoming and outgoing trains. Complicating the operation was the fact that the tall, ornate wrought iron and glass facade had to be dismantled piece by piece and placed on a trestle by day and by night lowered onto freight cars for removal from the site. Structures abutting the property, such as tenements along Lexington Avenue, also were demolished so that the actual blasting and drilling could begin in earnest.

Despite the use of the most modern equipment available, drilling for such areas as the two-tiered terminal gallery proved onerous because of the existence of Manhattan granite in the subsurface. "At one point," notes Oliver Jensen, "the granite cropped up 40 feet above street level forcing the old tracks to curve around the obstacle. Geologists were called in to lay out the drilling lines before the blasting."

Early in the planning the architects became aware that they desperately needed to increase the available space. By winning concessions from the city and purchasing nearby property, the railroad eventually was able to increase the total space available from 23 to more than 45 acres. More than a million cubic yards of earth and two million yards of granite were hauled away over a decade of excavation and construction. The result was a gaping hole in the middle of Manhattan which measured 40 feet deep, 770 feet wide and a half mile long. Given this space, the builders were to create a 32-track upper level for major trains such as the the Twentieth Century Limited, that plied the New York-Chicago run, and a 17-track lower level for the commuter lines which rolled to Westchester County and Connecticut. Wilgus's original formula called for a rather clever, and ultimately elaborate, link with the New York City Interborough Rapid Transit (IRT) subway, which had opened in 1904. The New York State Public Service Commission (PSC) had hoped to persuade a conventional railroad company, such as the New York Central, to take over the operating responsibility for the city subway system, but neither the New York Central nor any other railroad did so.

What did emerge was a plan for the expansion of the suburban Harlem and Hudson division commuter lines, and for these the railroad cleverly utilized razed iron and other debris as part of the refurbishing of the suburban routes.

"It was planned," wrote Wilgus, "that the yard excavation should be made in three successive 'bites,' each to be completed before the other was undertaken, working westward from Lexington Avenue, so that the traffic of the three railroads using the terminal . . . might continue without hindrance."

The first "bite" included the additions to the property that had been purchased at a time when it was deemed necessary to add to the existing acreage. This "bite" included a portion along Lexington Avenue and the east side of the site. A number of buildings along Park and Lexington avenues had to be demolished to get this project in motion. After nine years it was still unfinished, although some 750,000 pounds of dynamite were detonated to pave the way for construction.

One of the major elements in the redesign of Grand Central was expansion of existing trackage to accomodate the ever-increasing number of trains. Trains approached the station over the four-track main line until they reached 57th Street, where they were now routed to a ten-track

The present-day Grand Central Station rose on the site of the original. This view looking north includes the automobile ramp which circles the station as well as the Pan Am Building rising starkly in the background. — Stan Fischler Collection

arrangement, of which six moved onto the upper level and four dropped to the commuter-oriented lower level. The tracks for the commuter lines were placed directly on the rock floor of the excavation.

Electrification of the New York Central commuter lines was finished in 1907 under the stewardship of Wilgus. Ironically, it was to play a part in his departure from the scene several years before he planned to leave. The problem developed three days after the electric commuter lines went into service.

On February 16, 1907, an electrified commuter train heading for White Plains and Brewster left Grand Central pulling five wooden cars. It moved north through Harlem and thence into the Bronx, powered by two T-class electric locomotives. As the train speeded around a curve near 205th Street, it jumped the tracks, causing four of the five cars to somersault into splintered wreckage. Twenty-three passengers perished.

The disaster prompted an immediate investigation, including the testing of the relatively new electric locomotives. But the intensive probe proved futile in terms of a definitive reason for the wreck.

During the post-wreck controversy Wilgus and the Central's vice-president and general manager, A.H. Smith, collided in public over the issue of responsibility for the accident. Shortly thereafter, Wilgus handed in his resignation. His was followed by that of George A. Harwood, chief engineer of electric zone improvements.

The construction of Grand Central itself was not without its tragedy. In December 1910 a switching operation — which involved moving a train onto a yard track near 50th Street so that its car-lighting gas supply could be renewed — caused more trouble. In those days, most of the rolling stock used Pintsch gas rather than electricity to illuminate the inside of the cars. As the train was being backed into position, it accidentally was pushed past a bumping post and severed a gas line. The leaking gas wafted its way into an adjoining power substation used for the New York Central's electrification. The ensuing explosion leveled the substation, flattened a trolley operating on a nearby street and shattered $25,000 worth of plate glass in nearby buildings. A total of ten people were killed and 100 seriously injured, which hastened the discontinuance of Pintsch gas and its replacement with electricity on the New York Central.

Meanwhile, the widely discussed new depot was rapidly emerging from the enormous cavities around Park Avenue, 50th Street and Lexington Avenue. One of the most talked about features of the main structure was the Grand Concourse and its curved ceiling. A French artist, Paul Helleu, won the honor of painting a mural for the ceiling, and he produced the zodiac in blue and gold and the middle region of the sky. The ceiling was graced with 2,500 stars in gold leaf on a field of cerulean blue. When the ceiling was displayed to the public, it was discovered that Helleu had mistakenly painted the galaxy *in reverse*; West being where East should have been! The *faux pas* gained wide publicity, much to the dismay of the New York Central.

"The ceiling," countered the Central's public relations department, "is purely decorative, it was never intended that a mariner should set his course by the stars at Grand Central."

When the terminal finally was opened to a select group of 2,000 guests on February 1, 1913, the raves far overwhelmed any nitpicking about the geography of the ceiling. More than 60 years later, writing in *Railroads In America*, Oliver Jensen observed, "Grand Central was and is one of the most successful stations ever built . . . beyond all that fine functionalism, the station is beautiful."

The New York Central was justifiably proud of its monument to railroading and boasted about the soon-to-open depot in a variety of ways. A full-page advertisement in *Harper's Weekly* described Grand Central as "The Terminal City." "It will embrace hotels and modern apartment houses, convention and exhibition halls, clubs and restaurants, and department stores and specialty shops. In short, practically every sort of structure or entertainment incident to the modern city . . . There are 42 tracks for through travel and 25 tracks for local trains, 33 miles in all within the Terminal, accomodating over 1,000 cars at one time."

The auspicious debut of the depot was not without its light moment. A.R. Whaley, general superintendent of the railroad's electric division, provided his colleagues with a laugh by presenting a receipt to George A. Harwood, the Central's construction boss. The receipt, not unlike one would receive at a corner grocery store, simply stated: "Received at the hands of GEO. A. HARWOOD one Grand Central Terminal." It was signed by Whaley, Miles and Bronson, superintendent of the electric division, and W.L. Morse, the terminal manager.

That the expanded Grand Central was needed was underlined by the mathematics provided by the New York Central's bookkeeping department. For the year 1900 some 106,000 trains and 13,600,000 riders passed through the railroad's premiere station. Within ten years the figures had leaped to 130,000 trains and more than 20,000,000 passengers annually. A decade later the numbers of passengers had climbed to a level of over 37,000,000.

The most succinct but complete analysis of the new Grand Central's value is provided by William D. Middleton in his book about the terminal:

"Certainly, in its operational features the new terminal, together with the railroad's new suburban electrification, constituted a remarkable improvement over those of the old. The electrification, of course, solved the hazardous operating problems that had been created in the Park Avenue tunnel by the smoke and gases of steam locomotives, and simultaneously eliminated a source of the most intense public disaffection with the railroad. The great improvement in

The panoramic view (below) of Grand Central's "Grand Concourse" with the information booth (above) in the background, center. — Stan Fischler Collection

operating flexibility afforded by both the availability of the terminal loops and the use of multiple unit electric suburban trains, as well as the greatly increased storage capacity provided by the enlarged, two-level terminal, substantially reduced the requirement for terminal switching and the volume of 'deadhead' empty equipment moves between Grand Central and the Mott Haven yard north of the Harlem River."

Without question, Grand Central Terminal, although its final cost of $72,000,000 was far in excess of original estimates, fulfilled the targets and dreams of its planners. It not only proved an efficient depot for transporting and accommodating passengers, but became a landmark, a figure of speech and even the subject of a network radio program on CBS in the 1940's and 1950's called "Grand Central Station."

Americans from Seattle to Brooklyn still describe a crowded scene by stating, "This place looks like Grand Central Station!" Stars of stage, screen and radio frequented the depot enroute to the west coast on the Central's posh 20th Century Limited (which later gained fame as a full-length film and a Broadway musical), while the average work-a-day white-collar types daily jammed the commuter lines wending their way to Westchester and Connecticut.

On one occasion, at least, the office folk and the stars had their platforms inadvertently exchanged. The blunder developed when a Grand Central towerman mistakenly switched the 20th Century Limited onto a track used by commuter trains. The *grande dame* of the railroad then entered the depot on the lower level.

The tower then switched a commuter train to the upper level normally reserved for the 20th Century. Startled commuters found themselves treated like royalty. A red carpet was laid out, and a phalanx of red caps awaited. Meanwhile, on the level below, the high-class patrons were greeted by a murky platform devoid of the usual amenities.

Although the terminal was originally designed to handle more long-distance trains than commuter runs, it is the commuters, as William Middleton noted, who "have always been the real life-blood of Grand Central." By the late 1970's the numbers of long-range passenger trains had decreased sharply — even the 20th Century Limited was dead and buried. But commuter business continues to thrive as a major business of Grand Central.

Likewise, Grand Central has managed to survive several assaults against its elegance. One of the worst, according to Grand Central-philes who revere its Beaux-Arts design, was the construction of the huge, ugly 59-story Pan Am Building north of the terminal building in 1964. Equally disturbing was the erection of a huge, electrified billboard and a stockbroker's booth inside the main concourse. The most depressing threat of all — and one repeated several times since the end of World War II — was the possibility that the depot would be razed and replaced by a "modern" office building.

In 1969 the Penn Central Company, born of the merger of the New York Central and Pennsylvania railroads, supported the plan for a 55-story office building above the terminal. The idea prompted formation of a Save Grand Central Committee, which included among its supporters such notables as Jimmy Breslin, Jacqueline Kennedy Onassis and Bess Myerson. The battle raged through the 1970's with the New York City Landmarks Preservation Commission on the side of the Committee.

Ultimately, the Save Grand Central supporters prevailed and the plan for the skyscraper was defeated. Today, Grand Central Terminal remains, as one observer has noted, "precious and irreplacable, our greatest monument to what has been called the age of heroic materialism."

SECTION III: DISASTERS

CHAPTER 11:
NEW YORK AND NEW HAVEN RAILROAD, MAY 6, 1853

In the first years of railroading it was virtually impossible for a fatal accident to occur, simply because the small steam engines were only capable of pulling the tiny trains at slow speeds. A derailed locomotive might continue its momentum after leaving the track, but not for very long, nor with any dire consequences.

The first American railroad fatality of any kind occurred on June 17, 1831, on the South Carolina Railroad, when its pioneer locomotive, *The Best Friend of Charleston*, exploded, killing the engine fireman, a slave. The blast was caused when the fireman, annoyed by the loud hissing of steam escaping from the safety valve, held the valve down to stop the noise. This proved to be *finis* for both the fireman and *The Best Friend of Charleston*.

On November 8, 1833, a Camden and Amboy train carrying former President John Quincy Adams and the young Cornelius Vanderbilt caught fire in a wheel housing and jumped the tracks. James C. Steadman, a jeweler from Raleigh, North Carolina, had the dubious distinction of becoming the country's first passenger fatality. Adams escaped without injury, but was shaken by the accident. Vanderbilt suffered serious injury, which prompted an aversion to railroad traffic for many years until, ironically enough, he became one of the country's greatest rail magnates.

The first commuter train disaster did not occur until nearly 20 years later, when a New York and New Haven train ran off an open drawbridge at South Norwalk, Connecticut.

From the very beginning of railroading, planners were confronted with laying tracks over small bodies of water. To do so, rail builders frequently relied on a design which, by the end of the 1840's, was known as the standard railroad bridge. Designed by William Howe, the standard — or Howe — bridge was a rectangular frame of wooden diagonals and vertical iron tie rods. Although considered a cause of several accidents because of flawed design, the Howe bridge remained in vogue through the 1860's.

Rail historian Lucius Beebe suggests that the Howe truss caused as many train wrecks as did derailments. Drawbridges produced a corresponding peril — that one would somehow remain open when a train approached, causing the locomotive and cars to plunge into the water below. To prevent such a calamity from occurring, bridge builders and railroad men devised an assortment of regulations to ensure that trains never entered an open drawbridge. However, none of the precautions could atone for human failure. According to Robert C. Reed in *Train Wreck*, "The major danger for trains at drawbridges simply was the engineer's disregard of all warning signals."

Such was the case on April 23, 1853, when one of the Camden and Amboy engineers missed a stop signal as he approached the drawbridge at Rancocas Creek. The two o'clock train out of Philadelphia plunged into the creek. Miraculously, nobody was killed. Less than two weeks later, a New York and New Haven train suffered the same fate at South Norwalk, Connecticut, but with more tragic consequences.

The doomed train departed its terminal at Canal Street, New York City, at 8 a.m., May 6, 1853, enroute to New Haven. The engineer piloting the express to New Haven, one Edward Tucker, had put in four years service on the New York and New Haven, but not without blemish. In January 1851 he had been engineer on a train involved in a head-on collision at Mamaroneck, New York. Blame in that case was placed with the conductor, who apparently had persuaded Tucker that the track was clear because he — the conductor — had wired ahead that their train was en route. But a New York-bound train was on the same track.

Tucker just barely escaped death. After a lengthy hospitalization he gave up railroading to join California's gold rush, but that produced nothing but dirt for Tucker, so he returned East and re-applied for a job with the New York and New Haven. He was given employment as a *relief* engineer. On May 6, 1853, Tucker was pressed into service to take the express from lower Manhattan to New Haven. Tucker's conductor sounded the warning before the train had rolled out of the New York City limits: "Watch out for the red ball at the Norwalk (Connecticut) bridge."

The Norwalk drawbridge, like many on the New York and New Haven line, was erected to cross a broad river estuary emptying into Long Island Sound, in this case over the Norwalk River at South Norwalk, Connecticut. For safety's sake, on the open span the railroad had installed a large red ball approximately the size of a basketball on a pole by the track in front of the bridge. As a boat approached the span, the bridge tender was required to lower the red ball, thereby indicating that the engineer should bring his train to a full stop.

Tucker digested the warning from his conductor and then addressed himself to more imminent problems, such as reacquainting himself with the tracks ahead. The passengers, meanwhile, made themselves comfortable — including at least 29 doctors returning from a meeting of the American Medical Association in Manhattan.

The intinerary included stops at Stamford and Bridgeport en route to the big station in New Haven. The express was *not* to stop at the smaller Norwalk station, situated *before* — nearly 1,000 feet west — the drawbridge span and therefore a landmark forewarning Tucker to check out the bridge signal.

Under ideal conditions, an engineer in a New Haven-bound train could detect the large red ball even before reaching the Norwalk station. If, however, the signal was obstructed by trees in leaf, it was next visible from a point approximately 550 feet from the bridge. This meant that if an express was near its normal running speed of about 30 miles per hour after rounding the curve that preceded the bridge, the engineer would have to be vigilant in order to bring his train to a safe stop. Apparently Tucker was less than alert.

Shortly after 10:15 a.m., the steamboat *Pacific* had passed through the open drawbridge. A sufficient number of witnesses later testified that the bridge operator had lowered the ball into the "Stop!" position to make it fairly certain that Tucker was lying when he later testified that he had seen an all-clear signal.

The bridge operator recalled lowering the red ball from the 40-foot pole and placing it on a bridge base. He then set in motion the steam engine which slowly opened the 60-foot span. Not long after the *Pacific* had chugged through the gap, the New Haven Express could be heard in the distance.

Tucker's fireman, George Elmer, testified that he had no knowledge of the danger signal's position, since he was firing the engine at the time. "It was not my duty to look for it," Elmer answered before a jury.

Tucker steamed up to and past Norwalk station at a speed estimated at approximately 20 miles per hour and approached the wide-open span as if the drawbridge were closed and crossable. He realized the situation too late. With 370 feet of track between his locomotive and the gap, the frantic engineer leaped for the whistle cord and pulled twice, alerting his brakemen that an emergency was upon them.

The brakemen manning the coaches immediately behind the locomotive could see the dearth of track between them and the water, and they jumped, never putting hand to brake wheels. The brakemen on the last three coaches, however, remained at their stations and desperately swung the brakes into position. It was a heroic effort that undoubtedly saved dozens of lives in the rear cars.

Tucker's last-second emergency measures proved futile. "The speed of the train," said Robert C. Reed, "carried the engine clear across the channel into the central pier of the bridge. A baggage car, two mail cars, and two passenger coaches fell into the river." The third passenger coach first teetered on the brink, then split in half. A witness to the catastrophe later recounted the episode as follows: "The third passenger car snapped like a match; the flooring, the sides and the foremost end flying forward, with a jerk half across the draw. Many of the seats and the dislodged window sashes, with a crowd of timber fragments, were impelled, some of them fully across the gulf, and two of the passengers, who were seated just at the spot where the car snapped asunder, were thrown full twenty feet forward and pitched with frightful force upon the ruins of the second and first cars."

The *New York Daily Times* reported that the train was travelling at such an excessive rate of speed "that the engine nearly leaped the draw, striking with tremendous violence against the wall on the opposite side."

Several witnesses testified at the coroner's investigation which was held at the Norwalk railroad depot. O.S. Ferry, a Norwalk resident, delivered the following testimony:

"I was standing within 20 rods of the drawbridge. When the train came along, I had a full view of both the train and bridge; the train was going at full speed, so much so that the locomotive bounded over to the opposite pier or abutment of the draw. I think the draw master was not in the least to blame."

Witness after witness insisted that the ball (signal) was down and that there was no slackening of speed as the train approached the span. George G. Whistler, superintendent of the New Haven Railroad, testified that the engineer, Edward Tucker, had been involved in a collision at Greenwich, Connecticut, a year earlier, and had been censured for his failure to obey the conductor. Whistler further asserted that under normal conditions Tucker should have been able to avert a disaster. "He could see the bridge signal, near the little cut west of the bridge; he could even see the signal before reaching the depot when coming from New York; had the train been going 10 miles an hour, it could have been stopped before making the draw, had he noticed the signal."

One witness recalled hearing "one scream uttered simultaneously by many voices." Others remembered heartrending shrieks and the "crash of breaking timbers." Rescue operations began just moments after the express plunged into the Norwalk River. A growing number of spectators turned surly as they learned that the engineer and firemen had escaped injury by leaping from the doomed express. There were angry remarks that Tucker should be immediately shot or hanged.

Fortunately, a number of the doctors who had come from the medical convention survived the disaster and set about the business of comforting and treating the injured, including colleagues (five of the doctors died and 15 were injured in the crash). Many of the victims were hopelessly penned inside the submerged coaches. Forty-six passengers perished in what was by far the worst American railroad disaster up to that time.

News of the disaster spread from north to south and all points west. Within a day of the accident, Norwalk was jammed with friends and relatives of passengers who had been aboard the doomed train. One newspaper dispatch from Norwalk recounted the post-crash horror as follows:

"The scenes which ensued were of the most heartrending description. Numbers could be observed bending over the dead, weeping in frantic grief; others were hunting from house to house in search of a wounded mother, father, brother, sister, husband, or wife; and, up to the arrival of the latest train at Norwalk, it was estimated that over 2,000 persons had arrived there for this one sad purpose."

Lacking the sophisticated undersea rescue equipment of the 1980's, search parties in Norwalk labored slowly but surely to find survivors among the ruined passenger cars. "Few of the bodies taken out dead were bruised or disfigured," noted a *New York Daily Times* dispatch from the scene. "They presented a ghastly appearance, and in some instances, their clothing was literally torn to pieces. The remains were deposited in the railroad station house as fast as they were taken from the water. Most of them were placed in coffins."

Among the more bizarre episodes recounted was that of an infant in the care of an aunt, who was taking the child to its parents in Springfield, Massachusetts. The aunt was killed in the crash, but the infant survived.

Local residents, officials and state politicians demanded action. Investigations began at the grassroots level of the Norwalk Justice of the Peace and went as high as the Connecticut House of Representatives and State Senate. Some of the most vituperative orations were delivered by a Connecticut state representative who denounced engineer Tucker in the state's General Assembly.

"I will not call it accident," shouted this legislator. "I denounce it as wholesale, bloody, murderous massacre. In my opinion, the wretch whose brutal heedlessness or ignorance caused it should be hung on a gibbet higher than Haman's, and exposed to the scorn and execration of outraged humanity."

Enginner Tucker survived the threats of mob violence at the scene of the open bridge, but barely escaped the wrath of those who heard him deny that the ball was in the "Stop" position. One witness after another angrily announced that the red ball was, in fact, lowered and that Tucker was, to be generous, in error. The local jury of inquest at Norwalk, after hearing considerable testimony, ruled that Tucker was guilty of gross negligence. The verdict asserted, "In running around the curve at such a rapid rate, and under such circumstances, we think him guilty of the most criminal recklessness. At the same time we do not think the entire responsibility of this disaster rests upon him."

The latter portion of the verdict hinted that the New York and New Haven Railroad was to share in the guilt for not strictly enforcing speed regulations in the vicinity of the Norwalk River Bridge. Conductor Charles Comstock was charged with failure to alert Tucker that the express was exceeding speed limits as it approached the drawbridge.

Although the coroner's inquest into the slaughter held Tucker primarily responsible for the tragedy, state investigators probed more deeply into precisely what the New York and New Haven was doing to insure the safety of its passengers. The Connecticut House of Representatives and Senate concluded that the railroad must bear responsibility for the wreck.

Public wrath inspired the Connecticut Legislature to push through a bill calling for a Board of Railroad Commissioners. The New York and New Haven Railroad, to ensure that a repeat of the Norwalk tragedy never occurred, instituted a regulation requiring all trains to be halted completely before proceeding across *any* drawbridges on the line.

CHAPTER 12: DOUBLE DISASTER ON THE LONG ISLAND RAIL ROAD, 1950

By 1950 the Long Island Rail Road, "The Route Of The Dashing Commuter," was probably the most wretched, ineptly operated, high-density commuter line on the continent. Even some Long Island Rail Road officials privately admitted that. But their excuse, simply put, was that the Long Island had precious little money with which to make necessary repairs. Maintenance was deferred to the point of hazard. Rolling stock, for the most part, was more suitable for a museum than daily runs to Nassau and Suffolk counties. Criticism notwithstanding, the Long Island plodded along, bothering and bewildering its customers but managing, somehow, to avoid a catastrophe. It wasn't easy, not when the bankrupt line was carrying more than 400,000 passengers a day from its two terminals — Flatbush Avenue, Brooklyn, and Pennsylvania Station in Manhattan.

Despite innumerable shortcomings the Long Island went about its day-to-day business. Wherever funds could be found for improvement objects, patch work was done.

In February 1950, in cooperation with the town of Rockville Centre (Nassau County), the railroad was eliminating a troublesome grade crossing, choosing to install a simple gantlet. The gantlet is a stretch of track where two lines of track overlap so that one rail of each track is within the rails of the other. Because of this arrangement it is impossible to run more than one train over the gantlet without a collision.

While not the most sophisticated of railroads, the Long Island did take some precautions to avoid a head-on collision. When, for example, a train departed Rockville Centre Station en route to Manhattan or Brooklyn, proceeding to the gantlet, two warning signals were instantly flashed on the other side of the gantlet to prevent trains bound for the station and beyond from simultaneously crossing the gantlet. The first warning signal for motormen approaching Rockville Centre was placed 4,000 feet before the gantlet. It was situated to enable a motorman to come effectively to a stop before reaching the second — and last — signal before the gantlet.

Just a trifle more than 170 feet ahead of the gantlet the Long Island had installed its second warning device, a "home" signal. Orchestrating the arrivals and departure machinery was signal-block operator Charles Zablocki, who manned the controls at Rockville Centre on the night of February 17, 1950. Unlike his counterparts on the New York City subway system, Zablocki was at a disadvantage in that he had no effective power over human failure. If Zablocki flashed a "Stop" signal to a train from New York City approaching the Rockville Centre gantlet, he could only *hope* that the motorman would obey the lights, whereas on the New York City subways, automatic trippers would throw the emergency brakes on any train which ran a "Stop" signal.

At 10:30 p.m. on that Friday evening there was no reason for Zablocki to assume there would be problems in the moments ahead. It was a clear winter evening, unhampered by fog, rain, sleet or snow. Zablocki was addressing his attention to a pair of trains, one which would leave Rockville Centre for New York City and the other which had departed Pennsylvania Station en route to Babylon in Suffolk County. To reach its destination, the Babylon train would have to roll through Rockville Centre after crossing the gantlet.

The Manhattan-bound train was numbered 175 and operated by motorman James W. Markin. It had departed Babylon at 9:58 p.m. and was scheduled to leave Rockville Centre at 10:34 p.m. Coming in the opposite direction was Train Number 192, operated by Jacob Kiefer. An express, Kiefer's train had departed Pennsylvania Station at 10:03 p.m. The train operated by Kiefer and the eastbound Long Island unit were just minutes apart when Zablocki prepared to arrange the signals for Train Number 175 to leave Rockville Centre, and warn Markin to proceed with caution over the gantlet. Markin was dumbfounded by the sight of Kiefer's 12-car express hurtling at him at what appeared to be considerably more than a cautionary speed. Not only had the Babylon-bound train sped past the first warning signals, its momentum clearly indicated that there was no way the motorman would be able to bring it to a halt before it swung onto the gantlet. Testifying at a later probe, Markin recalled the final seconds before impact: "I saw him coming right down on top of me. I'd say he was about forty feet away. I was going about twelve of fifteen miles an hour at the time. I blew my alarm whistle and dimmed my headlight and threw on the brake."

Ironically, disaster could have been averted had Markin been disobeying regulations and taking his train through the gantlet at a higher speed. The extra acceleration might have enabled him to clear the temporary track before the Babylon Express swung from the normal track to the gantlet.

Markin's eight-car consist had just begun to swerve right, rolling out of the gantlet, when the eastbound train burst into the curve at approximately 30 to 35 miles per hour. Because the tracks were braided at that point — two distinct pair of tracks paralleling each other on the same set of ties — the trains collided, though not on the same tracks. Thus, the left portions of both cars bore the brunt of impact, while the right (motorman's) side received less of the blow.

At the moment of collision, the report of steel ramming steel sent reverberations throughout the normally sleepy community of Rockville Centre. The initial tremor caused by the collision was followed by piercing screams and frightening, lightning-like electric flashes from the disrupted third-rail. Adding to the chaos was the tragic fact that the first cars of both trains were more crowded than the others because it was Long Island policy to maintain the lead and last coaches for smokers.

Twenty-nine passengers perished almost instantly. (Rescuers picking their way through the wreckage found victims piled five deep). Many were saved, but three of the more seriously injured passengers later died from wounds suffered in the crash. The motormen of both destroyed trains survived without serious injury — due, no doubt, to the fact that their cabs were away from the points of contact — and were available for interrogation soon after the Nassau County District Attorney's office launched its probe.

Depending upon their placement in the cars, passengers gave varying accounts of the crash. Paul Back, a 21-year-old Brooklyn College student, who was on the eastbound train, gave the following account of the wreck to the Associated Press:

"There was a tremendous shock. My head hit the wall and the lights went out in all the cars. I got up and walked toward the exit door and heard screams for help. So, I started to investigate the westbound train. There were a lot of people around seriously cut and hurt — broken bones and so forth. One man was screaming 'Kill me, please kill me.' He thought his back was broken.

"Another woman, pinned down in the middle of the first car, screamed: 'Get the weight off me.' It was about ten minutes before the first doctors and firemen arrived. I didn't see any fire at all. The head car of the westbound train was split in two; one side of it was sheared off. A woman fell through the front door but we brought her back in and calmed her down."

In the early morning hours a number of clergymen of various faiths moved among the wreckage, comforting the wounded. One priest stood by in a wrecked car as a double amputation was performed upon a man. A general appeal went out for welders in the area to help free those either dead or injured pinned inside the trains. More than two hours after the impact, more than a dozen persons were still pinned beneath the steel cars.

In the middle of the night the emergency crew probed the wreckage of the Rockville Centre disaster which involved almost 1000 passengers.
— Stan Fischler Collection

The horror of the stricken Long Island Rail Road train is shown as both injured and dead are confronted by rescuers at Rockville Centre.   — Stan Fischler Collection

The impact of the Long Island trains colliding at Rockville Centre, N.Y. was so awesome that one of the cars was sheared in half.
— Stan Fischler Collection

The still smoldering upside down Long Island Rail Road coach is mute testimony of one of the worst disasters in New York commuting history.

The catastrophic melding of Long Island Rail Road cars is evident as the inside of the coach on the left was caved in by the train on the right.

– Stan Fischler Collection

Workmen inspect the devastated Long Island Rail Road coach in the morning after the February 17th, 1950 wreck in Rockville Centre, N.Y. A crane clears debris in the background.
— Stan Fischler Collection

Reacting quickly to the accident report, the Long Island Rail Road cut off power on its third rail to prevent electrocutions. Meanwhile, the American Red Cross established emergency headquarters nearby at the Second Baptist Church.

District Attorney Frank Gulotta confronted motorman Markin but soon released him and asserted that no charges would be filed, ostensibly because he had followed his orders to the letter. By contrast, Kiefer faced long periods of questioning and a trial. To all, the most perplexing question was why Kiefer moved his express through not one but two warning signals prior to entering the gantlet?

Kiefer explained that soon after the Babylon Express had cruised past the Lynbrook Station he ceased functioning as an alert motorman. "I don't remember anything until I was at the bottom of the hill, a few seconds before the crash," said Kiefer before the court. "When I came to, I saw the signal was against me. I heard my cab control whistle blowing and I saw the other train coming. I was only a couple of hundred feet west of the stop signal."

The motorman then explained that he put his brake into emergency position before the trains collided. The prosecuting attorney attempted to depict Kiefer as reckless and insensitive to the peril in which he placed his passengers, but the jury was persuaded by the doctor testifying on behalf of Kiefer that his patient apparently had suffered "from a spasm of the blood vessels in the brain that resulted in unconsciousness for that period." Kiefer's lawyer added that it would be absurd to believe that his client would deliberately have allowed the train to rampage unbraked down the grade when the motorman, himself, was threatened with injury or even death. It was a persuasive argument, and the jury ruled motorman Kiefer not guilty of criminal negligence and second-degree manslaughter.

Soon after the wreck LIRR officials promised to place a system of manual safety tripping devices at the gantlet. Once the trippers were in place the New York State Public Service Commission ordered the Long Island to inform all motormen that trains must slow to a speed of 15 miles per hour when they reached a point 600 feet from the gantlet. It was, of course, too late. Thirty-two passengers were dead and 76 others were recovering from injuries. There were no further problems at the gantlet, but the Long Island Rail Road had not experienced its only disaster of 1950. A second was to happen nine months later, on November 22, 1950, in the borough of Queens.

It was the very height of irony that another Babylon Express was cast as the culprit in what developed into one of the worst tragedies in commuter rail history. This time the site was several miles closer to Manhattan. The main line of the Long Island traces a scenic route as it sprints along an embankment through Forest Hills, Kew Gardens, and then Richmond Hill, all in Queens.

Early in the evening of November 22, 1950, motorman William M. Murphy was piloting a jammed train bound for Hempstead in Nassau County. It was Thanksgiving Eve. The old steel cars rolled smartly through the East River tunnel, past Woodside and Elmhurst, with Forest Hills looming ahead. The business district of Continental Avenue was bustling with shoppers as Murphy prepared to check the signals at Union Turnpike, the next major thoroughfare on the run through Queens. A 31-year veteran of the line, Murphy had become accustomed to delays, so it was no surprise to him that the lights on the signal bridge which extended over the main line warned him to slow down to no more than 30 miles per hour.

Murphy grabbed the steel brake handle and pulled it forward, causing a hiss of the air brakes and a slight lurch as the curved brake shoes pressed against the wheels. To the passengers, this change of speed made little impression, since trains on the heavily travelled route frequently slowed to a crawl during rush hours. Nor was it surprising that Murphy slowed the train even more when he detected the "Restricted" signal ahead at Metropolitan Avenue in Richmond Hill.

Again, Murphy pushed the brake handle, then moved it back and forth to obtain a smoother deceleration. The signal warned that the train should not exceed 15 miles per hour. Murphy already had the train slow enough to satisfy the regulation and now moved the brake handle into the off position so that his train could cruise until the next signal. But when the motorman released — or thought he had by pushing the brake handle into the free position — the steel brake shoes continued to hug the wheels, forcing the Hempstead-bound train to stop at Metropolitan Avenue.

Frustrated, Murphy was further infuriated when he saw the signal light change into a new position, allowing him to move the train at 30 miles per hour. Try as he might, Murphy was unable to unlock the brakes.

Since the Hempstead train was sitting on the main line, and since other trains frequented the express tracks, it was now imperative that rudimentary safety precautions be taken to insure that any other train on the same track was aware that the Hempstead consist was immobilized. Brakeman Bertram Biggam picked up a red warning lantern, unlocked the rear door of the train and clambered down to the tracks. It was cold. Biggam was pleased when he heard the electic motor of the train humming. It suggested that the brake problem was only temporary and that Murphy would soon have the coaches moving again.

But this was not the case. Biggam hoped no other trains would appear. But as he unlocked the rear door of the Hempstead train, he looked up in horror to see the high beam of the front light of the Babylon Express bearing down upon him on the same track as his Hempstead train. Hopeless as it seemed, Biggam nevertheless made a last-ditch effort to communicate with the onrushing Babylon Express. He waved his red lamp until it was impossible for him to wave it anymore.

Why was the Babylon Express suddenly in a position to pulverize his train? The only person qualified to provide a definite answer was Benjamin J. Pokorny, pilot of the Babylon Express and well-acquainted with the Long Island's tracks, signals and general operations. A veteran of the line, Pokorny had pulled the controller in his cab into the starting position five minutes after Murphy had taken the Hempstead train through the East River tunnel.

For Pokorny it was clear rolling into Long Island City, through Rego Park and Forest Hills. According to crew members on the Babylon Express, Pokorny did, in fact, slow his train as it entered the block signal area. Pokorny was not ony observing but adhering to the signal regulations. There was, however, a catch. Pokorny was in position to see clearly the signal lights on the steel bridge that spanned the main line and therefore able to see the movement of the lights change from the "Restricted Speed" position to "Approach." But these were the signals given to Murphy's Hempstead train, which Pokorny, under normal circumstances, would correctly have assumed had moved on.

So it was not surprising that the Babylon Express, after having slowed down, suddenly moved back into a higher speed (about 35 miles per hour) within striking distance of the stalled train ahead. Pokorny no doubt moved his controller into the higher speed upon seeing the signal change from "Restricted Speed" to "Approach." But wouldn't Pokorny, like any other engineer, have seen the red emergency lanterns ahead or, at the least, the rear platform lights of a train in his tracks?

While it is true that brakeman Biggam waved his red lantern when the Babylon Express sped into view, the sight of that flickering light would have given Pokorny precious little time to set his emergency brakes. One who watched, first in curiosity and then in horror, was Fred Mergi, a passenger in the last car of the Hempstead train. When Biggam re-opened the rear door to re-check the tracks ahead, Mergi, a fireman by profession, looked back to see what was the matter. He was as horror-stricken by what he saw, as was Biggam. "This big white light flooded the car and we (he and Biggam) both went for the floor," said Mergi. "I was lucky and slid down the aisle. The lights went out and glass crashed. Everybody was yelling and screaming. A chandelier came crashing down on my head."

The 12-car Babylon Express, at the high rate of speed it was travelling, had no chance to decelerate in time to avert a collision. As engineer Pokorny gaped in horror, the Express struck the Hempstead train from behind with such force that it sheared through the bottom of the rear car, lifting it off the tracks and, horrifically, piggy-back style on top of the first car of the Babylon Express, which came to a stop amid a cacophony of shrieks and moans. So powerful was the impact that the lead car of the Babylon train telescoped through all but five feet of the rear car of the Hempstead train.

Several residents of homes adjoining the railroad tracks rushed to the crash scene and tended the injured. One man who helped carry victims to homes in the vicinity for treatment was Harold Coyle, a Kew Gardens (Queens) tavern owner. "The crash," said Coyle, "sounded like an explosion. It shook the house. I ran to the tracks and heard groans. An aluminum train was underneath another one. In other cars — they looked crowded — people seemed to keep their seats for a moment and then try to leave. The injured kept asking 'Where am I?' and 'What happened?' as they were removed from the wreckage."

William H. Good, a member of the national advertising staff of *The New York Times*, was a passenger in the eighth car of the second train. "All of a sudden the brakes were jammed on," he remembered. "I was standing and was thrown down the aisle. Some glass was broken in my car but I don't think anybody was hurt. From the way our motorman threw on the brakes, I don't think he had any notice that the collision was coming. The first car was smashed to pieces. It plowed under the rear of the other."

Good related that there were no sounds emanating from inside the smashed cars. "I saw bloody hands hanging out of the windows," he recounted. "They must have been dead; all of them. At first glance I saw ten bodies."

Like many other homeowners, Mr. and Mrs. William Stoker were having dinner in their house, which sat just a stone's throw from the railroad tracks. They were startled by the unusual sounds which cut through the November evening.

"It sounded like an atomic bomb," said Mrs. Stoker. "I thought at first that the furnace had blown up. Then I ran outside, saw what happened and ran in to call the police and hospitals. But the ambulances didn't come fast enough and when the people started climbing out, I took two carloads to the hospital myself."

Among those most traumatized by the collision were passengers in the last car of the first train. Many of them had become aware of the impending disaster when the high beam of the speeding second train grew brighter and brighter inside the first train as it sped toward impact. Some terrified passengers in the doomed last car of the first train grabbed their seats for support, others dove to the floor, while still others were sleeping and had no idea that a collision was about to take place. Sherwood Faubel was one rider with no hint of a collision.

"I was snoozing," Faubel said, "but suddenly heard a loud noise. There was a terrific jolt and then I was thrown forward in my seat. Glass showered all over. People yelled and screamed. Some were covered with blood."

Faubel was temporarily immobilized until firemen arrived and turned on emergency lights. "They helped me out," he said. "I was lucky."

The New York Times reported that "white-coated doctors and ambulance attendants hurried from victim to victim administering morphine injections to those in pain and soothing the frightened with words of comfort. As the night wore on and the cold became more penetrating, the doctors and nurses draped blankets over their hospital attire."

Physicians claimed that two-thirds of the surviving injured owed their lives to the heroism of two young hospital interns, Dr. Paul E. Soffer and Dr. Arnold R. Sanders. The pair of medics squeezed their way between telescoped cars, where they worked for four-and-a-half hours, ministering to the trapped riders. Finally, the two young physicians crawled out and collapsed.

David George, a publicity representative of the Long Island Rail Road, was a passenger in the last car of the first eastbound train. When the crash occurred George was knocked to the floor of the car but survived the crash. "Our train made an emergency stop at 6:26 p.m.," said George. "Moments later there was a rending crash. I lost consciousness and when I came to my senses in

The ill-fated Long Island Rail Road suffered its second horrific catastrophe within a year in 1950 when an express plowed into a local at Kew Gardens, Queens on November 22, 1950. The express is seen piled upon the local as workmen, police, and onlookers are involved in the rescue operation.
— Stan Fischler Collection

To remove the telescoped express off the local, a huge railroad crane was required.
— Stan Fischler Collection

the darkness I heard the screams and cries for help from the trapped passengers. The few passengers remaining in the front of the car, assisted by the standees on the platform, made their way out of the train."

Accompanying George on the trip was Robert Patterson, assistant traffic manager of the Long Island Rail Road. When both had recovered from the impact, they swung into action. They scrambled down the embankment to a house where they could call for help.

Precisely when the motorman of the Babylon Express realized he was about to telescope his train into the rear of the Hempstead consist remains a moot point, for he perished in the crash. Commissioners of the Interstate Commerce Commission, who subsequently investigated the accident, concluded that Pokorny might not have seen any signal until he detected the desperate waving of brakeman Biggam's lantern. No matter how quickly he threw the emergency brake at that point, it was impossible to come even close to halting the onrushing express before impact. The proof of that is in the scene following the accident. So thoroughly telescoped was the Hempstead train that it appeared to be actually atop the Babylon Express as a top deck in a double-decker. Under the circumstances it was difficult to imagine that anyone in either the first car of the Babylon Express or last car of the Hempstead train could have survived this worst disaster in the history of the Long Island Rail Road. A total of 79 persons were killed and 363 injured as a result of the wreck.

Again, the public demanded to know why such a calamity could occur at a time when railroads had available to them the most modern safety technology. At the very least, the Long Island could have done what the New York City transit system had done long before: install safety trippers to throw the emergency brakes of any train that ran through a "Stop" signal. Astonishingly, the Long Island insisted that such trippers, while fine for municipal systems, were not applicable for "all-weather" commuter lines. Ultimately, the Interstate Commerce Commission rejected this line of reasoning and ordered the Long Island to install modern safety systems on 53 miles of tracks. A combination of Interstate Commerce Commission, Public Service Commission and local pressures compelled the reluctant Long Island to install modern automatic train-control systems that would have been effective deterrents to both 1950 disasters.

If nothing else, the two wrecks involving the Babylon Express focused attention on the need to upgrade LIRR safety. The changes came slowly, almost painfully, but by the 1960's there was a feeling that Long Island precautions were adequate to prevent further disasters like those of 1950.

The impact of the Kew Gardens crash of Long Island trains threw the speeding express directly atop the stalled local.
– Stan Fischler Collection

The wreck of "The Broker" marked the third major commuter disaster in the New York area in less than a year.

– Stan Fischler Collection

CHAPTER 13: THE BROKER DERAILS

Engineer Joseph H. Fitzsimmons knew that February 6, 1951, would not be a normal day in his life as a Pennsylvania Railroad engineer. A 57-year-old veteran of the Pennsy, Fitzsimmons was scheduled to pilot the 5:10 p.m. commuter train out of the Jersey City depot en route to the Jersey shore communities.

Fitzsimmons was accustomed to rush-hour traffic, but this was different. The Jersey Central Railroad, which normally served the townships near the Atlantic Ocean, had come to a standstill because of a strike, and many of the Central's customers had switched to the Pennsylvania. As a result, Fitzsimmons' 11-car consist was packed beyond all reason. Where normally a rider on the 5:10 — dubbed "The Broker" — could expect to find a seat for the trip south to the suburbs, this time commuters found themselves standing in the aisles like New York City subway straphangers.

The Broker was a special train in yet another way. Unlike most commuter runs which were powered either by electricity or diesel engines, *The Broker* was pulled by a traditional steam engine, and at 5:10 Fitzsimmons pulled on the throttle setting the huge drive wheels in motion. Standing against the seat backs, many of the passengers were jolted against each other as the venerable locomotive crossed the switches and headed for open track and its ultimate destination, Bay Head Junction. Then both passengers and crew settled into the anticipation of a relatively smooth, uneventful ride south. The only bump on the ride might occur at a tiny, makeshift trestle on the line less than half a mile south of Woodbridge Station. The trestle, necessary to accommodate construction being done on a nearby automobile roadway, had been put into operation that day.

No longer than a traditional railway coach, the trestle by its very nature presented problems in terms of normal flow of railway travel. For one thing, the trestle eliminated the straightaway, which meant that an approaching train first had to negotiate a five-degree curve before rolling over the temporary span.

To prevent its engineers from speeding into the curve on the trestle approach, the Pennsy dispatched a communique to all of its train crews more than a week before the interim spur was opened for traffic. The order reported that the trestle would begin accepting trains at 1:01 p.m. on February 6th, and that trains were to decelerate from their normal running speeds *to 25 miles per hour before reaching the curve and trestle*. What the Pennsylvania high command neglected to do, however, was take precautions to supplement the order and install some form of warning device, be it flashing lights or flags, on the tracks a safe distance before the five-degree curve. (Pennsy officials later maintained that the original directive, ordering trains to slow down before the temporary track, was sufficient within the context of the PRR's operating procedures.)

Although Fitzsimmons had previously worked on another railroad which *had* employed warning signals in similar circumstances, he was aware that the Pennsylvania did not provide such safeguards, as were his fireman, A.M. Dunn, and the conductor on *The Broker*, John H. Bishop. It is doubtful that any of the more than 1,000 riders on the overcrowded train were aware of the situation. Nor could they have known that the cab of the locomotive on *The Broker* did *not* have a speedometer!

Nevertheless, a veteran of railroading such as Fitzsimmons could instinctively determine the speed at which his engine was travelling. As for the January 29th PRR order about slowing down at Woodbridge, conductor Bishop reminded his engineer of this before the 11-car commuter train chugged out of its Jersey City terminal.

There was no moon in the sky as *The Broker* left Jersey City in the distance. On this midwinter evening, passengers wore their overcoats on the train. Many who worked in the business district of downtown Manhattan had placed their attache cases on the overhead storage rack. Others played cards, worked on crossword puzzles, read the evening paper, or just dozed. The unlucky latecomers, forced to stand, peered through the frosty windows of the aged pre-World War II cars at the blur of factories and homes that comprised the landscape of this industrial portion of New Jersey.

Of all the employees working *The Broker*, no one had a more difficult time than conductor Bishop. It was his job to move from seat to seat through the jammed train, collecting tickets, while handling an assortment of other duties. On this night the throngs lining the aisles made it difficult for the 34-year Pennsy veteran to make it through the cars.

Bishop, like any good railroad man, had made a mental note of the danger spot at Woodbridge and constantly recalled the special memorandum the railroad had earlier issued to all hands. If he was worried about the effectiveness of the detour, there was already ample proof that it worked. Prior to *The Broker*, no less than six trains had rolled to the five-degree curve, turned on to the temporary tracks and crossed the temporary bridge. They then swerved back to the regular main line tracks and continued on their way to Bay Head Junction. If the new orders were observed, there should be no problem negotiating the detour.

Nearly a half hour had elapsed when the conductor realized that Woodbridge was not far off. Nevertheless, *The Broker* steamed along with no signs that engineer Fitzsimmons had a mind to slow the 11-car train to the required 25-miles-per-hour limit at the Woodbridge trestle.

Conductor Bishop became alarmed with the train's speed. He knew that Woodbridge was mere minutes — if not precious seconds — away. He began to pray for the telltale hiss of the air brakes, or for the customary lurch of the cars as the brake shoes hugged the wheels. But nothing was forthcoming. It was time for the conductor to make his move.

Bishop's eye was on the red wooden handle hanging from an old grey cord above the seats at the end of the car. With luck, he would reach the emergency signal in time and yank it into the S.O.S. position, so that Fitzsimmmons would reduce speed to a sensible pace.

Meanwhile, in the cab Fitzsimmons appeared to be piloting his train as if it were an ordinary run. Later the engineer claimed that he was peering ahead in search of a warning signal. "All the time," Fitzsimmons asserted, "I was looking for a yellow light, a yellow light, a yellow light."

There was, of course, no yellow light.

Conductor Bishop never reached the emergency cord. *The Broker*, travelling at a speed far in excess of the 25 miles-per-hour ordered for the trestle approach, reached the curve at approximately 5:43 p.m. The wheels of the locomotive screamed as the flanges were hurled against the inside rim of the track. In a trice, the wheels climbed over the rail and, within a second or two, the wheels of the tender also went over, followed by the next eight cars of the train.

With the ear-splitting screech of steel against steel, the locomotive hurled itself across the bridge, its funnel still belching steam. Its momentum finally spent by the uneven track bed, the locomotive finally tipped over on its side with a last gasp. Fitzsimmons was lucky: he was hurled from his cab and survived the wreck with relatively minor injuries, but others were far less fortunate.

The tender uncoupled from its locomotive and careened down the PRR embankment to Fulton Street below. But the coupling between the tender and the first coach, as well as the coupling between the first and second coaches, held fast and the passenger cars grotesquely followed the tender down the hill. Worse was the fate of the third and fourth cars, which also

A phalanx of fire engines and ambulances converged on Woodbridge to rescue the rush-hour passengers involved in the Woodbridge wreck.
— Stan Fischler Collection

The makeshift wooden trestle with temporary walkway can be seen to the left of the derailed coaches at Woodbridge. — Stan Fischler Collection

Rescuers arrived on the scene almost immediately after the Woodbridge wreck took place, but often found they were helpless in attempts to save trapped passengers.
— Stan Fischler Collection

Two coaches which have passed over the temporary bridge (upper right rear) are jackknifed over the right of way at Woodbridge. — Stan Fischler Collection

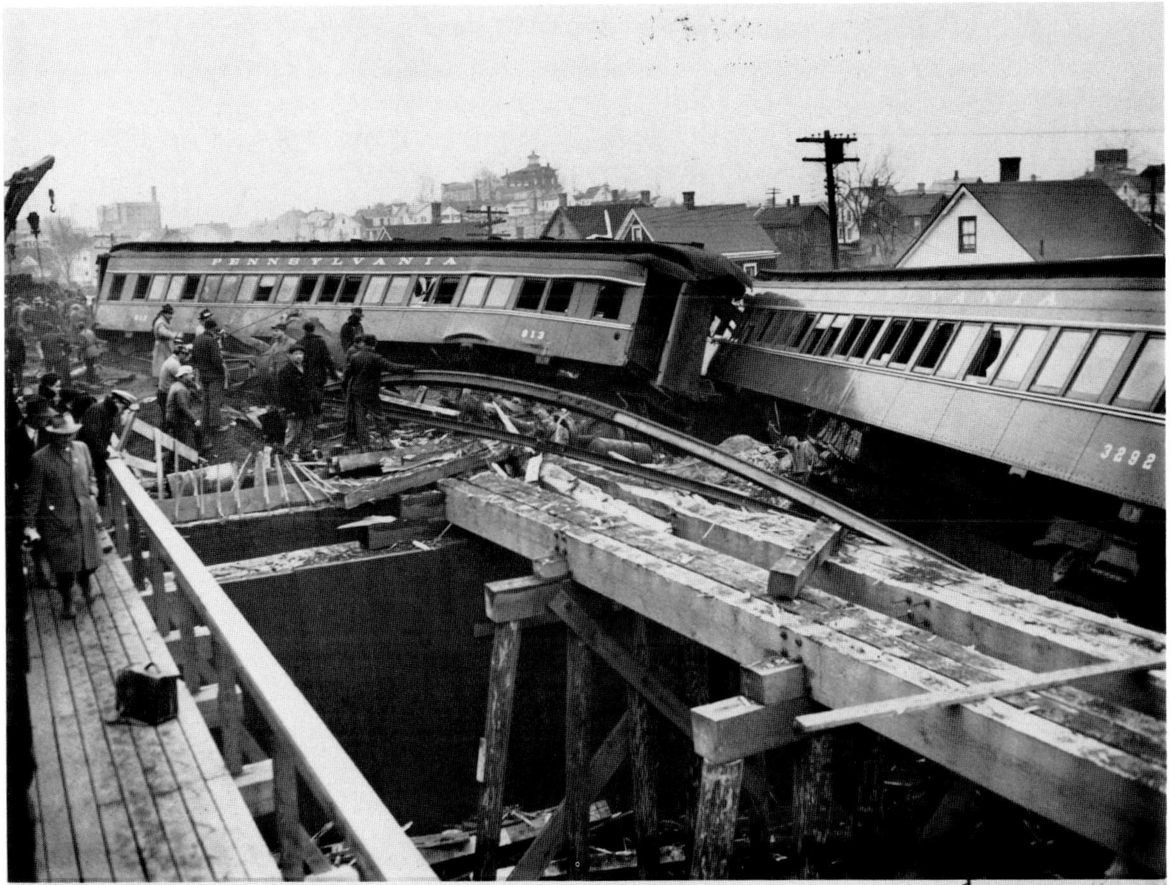
PENNSYLVANIA
813
3292

PENNSYLVANIA

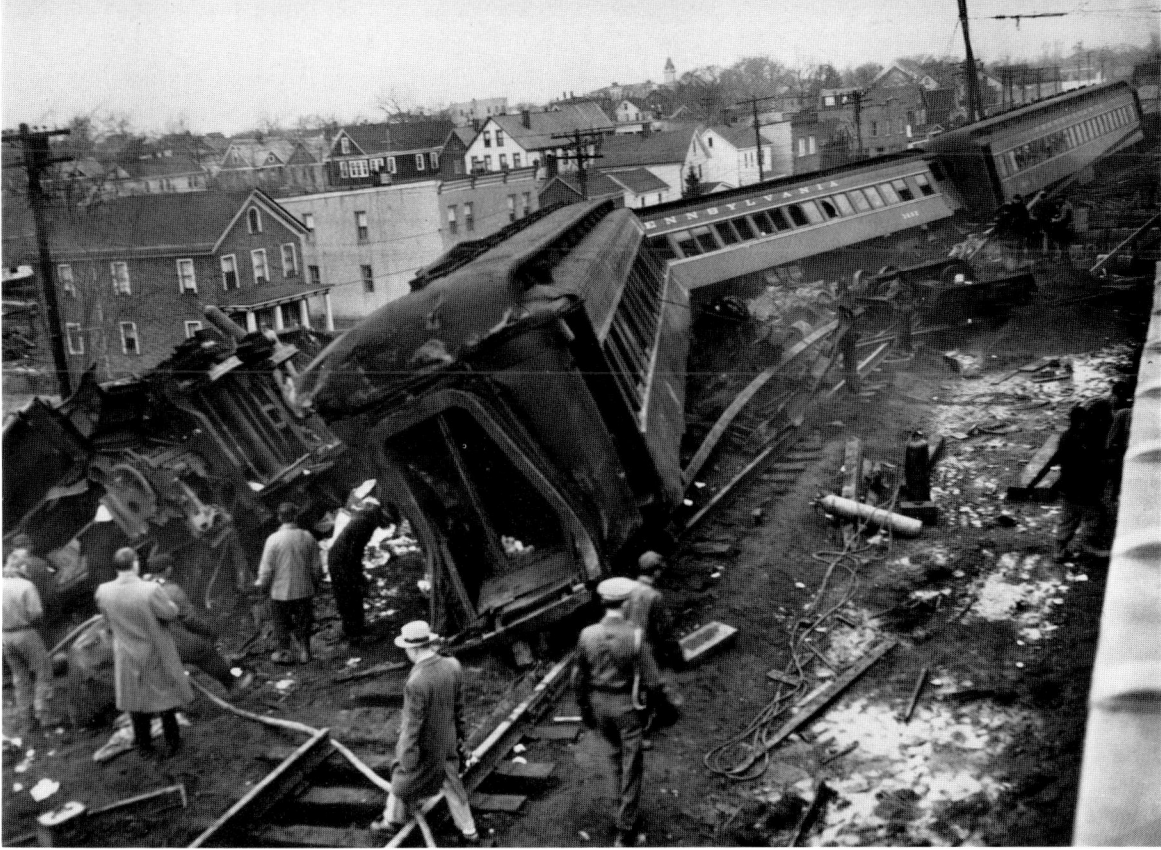

plunged to Fulton Street, but crumpled in the process like soda cans under stomping feet. The last three cars remained on the rails, their passengers watching in horror.

The scene was hardly comforting to the citizens of Woodbridge, who were startled at their dinner tables by the cacophony along the tracks. One housewife who lived within shouting distance of the trestle stood transfixed in her kitchen as she heard the crashing train. "It shook the house like jelly," she said. "I thought it was an earthquake."

The density of the passenger load multiplied the effects of the calamity. Survivors clambered wildly over the dead and dying in an effort to free themselves from the twisted steel and splintered wood. The normally sturdy coaches had burst apart under the impact and the twisting and pulling of converging forces.

After the initial thrust carried the equipment off the tracks and over the embankment, the metallic sounds of the disaster gave way to a hissing of steam mixed with the eerie shrieks of the wounded. Emergency calls were put through to all nearby hospitals and soon a corps of medical men, national guardsmen and train personnel were attempting to provide succor for survivors, while ensuring an orderly salvage of equipment.

A flock of newsmen descended upon Woodbridge, as well as investigators representing the railroad and local law enforcement agencies. For them the key witness was Engineer Fitzsimmons, who had been removed to Perth Amboy Hospital where his wounds ranged from scalp cuts to broken ribs. His fireman died of injuries in the same hospital less than two hours after the wreck. Questioned by investigators, Fitzsimmons at first insisted that he had held *The Broker* down to a reasonable speed before reaching the makeshift trestle: "I entered the trestle at about 25 miles an hour and the speed of the train certainly couldn't be blamed for the crash."

The engineer's story was immediately challenged by several passengers, one a PRR employee who countered that the train was rolling at a normal — not a restrained — speed when it hit the curve. Other witnesses suggested that the train was going as fast as 60 miles an hour, while others guessed it was travelling at 45 miles-per-hour In time engineer Fitzsimmons altered his original assertion and allowed that *The Broker* could well have been travelling faster than he had originally estimated.

When the final death toll from the wreck had soared to 84 persons (with 345 injured), public opinion swelled against the Pennsy for its failure to provide warning signals before the curve, to complement earlier written orders. The *New York Times* lambasted the railroad in an editorial: "Could not the railroad, which issued an admonitory bulletin more than a week in advance of the accident, have installed caution signals? Why didn't it do this? Who is to blame for its not being done?"

More than two months after the disaster, the Interstate Commerce Commission concluded in its report that the wreck was "caused by excessive speed on a curve of a temporary track."

As so often has been the case with railroad misfortune, some good came of this one, although at tremendous cost in human life. In the aftermath of the episode at Woodbridge, the Pennsy disclosed that it would implement a multi-million-dollar automatic speed control system, which, had it been in effect on February 6, 1951, would have prevented the loss of 84 lives.

CHAPTER 14: THE MYSTERY OF THE OPEN BRIDGE

George Stirnweiss was not your everyday straphanger on the Jersey Central's commuter Train No. 3314 to Jersey City. A native of New York City, "Snuffy" Stirnweiss, from 1943 until 1950, wore the pinstripe uniform of the New York Yankees, playing on three World Series winners. Although never a sports hero in the proportions of Joe DiMaggio, Stirnweiss nevertheless had become a New York favorite. Thus it was not unusual, eight years after hanging up his Yankee uniform the last time, for him to be hailed on the streets or on the daily commuter run to work.

September 15, 1958, was the Jewish New Year (Rosh Hashanah). The commuter train was less crowded than usual. The pair of 1,500-horsepower General Motors diesels pulled five ancient coaches out of Bay Head Junction, heading north along the shore to Asbury Park, Long Branch, Red Bank and Matawan. At Cranford Junction the tracks split with the old Lehigh Valley, switching left, while the regular Jersey Central headed right to Elizabethport, Bayonne and finally the venerable Jersey City passenger terminal, where New York-bound executives then boarded the ferry across the Hudson River to lower Manhattan.

Like other passengers Stirnweiss made the best of his rickety ride. As far as quality was concerned, the Jersey Central could not have cared less about its patrons. Already twice bankrupted, the line again tottered on the brink. The railroad's desperate state was betrayed by its rolling stock. The 100 passengers on Train No. 3314 were bounced toward Jersey City on equipment that had long been obsolete.

The lead locomotive, though hardly a relic, was lacking one safety device considered vital to operators of rapid transit and commuter railroads: the "dead-man" switch. On all New York City subway trains, for example, passengers and crew are protected by a device introduced in the 1920's which automatically brings the train to a halt if the motorman (engineer) suffers an attack and his hand drops from the controller (throttle). At this point the controller springs upward and, although the train may be at high speed, the dead-man switch instantly releases emergency brakes and halts the consist. This device was not only mandatory on the New York system, but was in use on trains throughout the continent. Yet Train No. 3314 out of Bay Head did not have a dead-man switch, despite the fact that other Jersey Central locomotives had such devices.

Lacking this fail-safe system, the engineer and fireman followed a Jersey Central procedure which called for them to vocalize each signal ahead. Thus, fireman Peter Andrews worked directly with his engineer, Lloyd Wilburn, as follows: When the 63-year-old engineer spotted a signal, he would call it out to his 42-year-old fireman, who then would verify it in a loud voice. Members of the Jersey Central high command later insisted that their word-of-mouth verification system was as "dependable" as the dead-man switch.

Since Train No. 3314 traversed some of the metropolitan area's more affluent suburbs, it was not surprising that the passenger list included the cream of assorted New Jersey communities. Shrewsbury (New Jersey) Mayor John Hawkins was aboard, as well as Elton Clark, a director of the gigantic Allied Chemical Corporation. In addition there was Mrs. Florence Geogarty, chairperson of the board of a freight forwarding and brokerage company, and Mrs. Rafael Leon, whose husband was a financier from Venezuela.

Clark and Hawkins were in the second coach, along with Stirnweiss, when the train left Elizabethport on schedule. From here the run to Bayonne could be quick or agonizingly long: it all hinged upon the action at Jersey Central's Newark Bay Bridge. The four-track, one-and-one-half-mile long span was as big as railroad lift bridges went and, to the irritation of Jersey Central commuters, it did the job for which it was intended — in spades.

Increased ship traffic in Newark Bay meant that the pair of 150-foot draws and the four tracks were being raised so often that trains were regularly delayed while ships passed through the opening. Railroaders were angered by the bridge because of the time consumption and shippers loathed it as a navigational hazard.

Since the Newark Bay Bridge was lifted a minimum of 25 times daily on weekdays, the Jersey Central was compelled to invoke stringent and complicated safety precautions to prevent its trains from rolling up to an open span. Wesley S. Griswold recalls them in his book *Train Wreck*.

"Three signal lights were spaced along each railroad approach to the bridge. They were located three-quarters of a mile, a quarter of a mile, and 500 feet from the draws. When the bridge was open, the two lights farthest from it shone amber; the third glowed red. Jersey Central rules required a train approaching these signals to start slowing down from a customary 45 mph if the first light was amber, reduce speed to between 15 and 20 mph if the second light was amber, and, of course, stop at the third light if it was red. In the extremely unlikely event that a train should run past all three signals, an automatic derailing device 50 feet beyond the red light was set to throw it off the track to the crossties, which presumably would halt it. Signal lights and derailer functioned automatically when the bridge lifted. Conversely, unless the signals and derailer were working properly, the draws could not be opened."

Based on their experience as railroaders, there was no reason to suspect that engineer Wilburn or fireman Andrew were anything but safety-conscious employees. Although he was advanced in age (63), Wilburn had recently passed his physical with flying colors. Fireman Andrew had been advised to restrict his duty because of "moderate elevation of blood pressure."

Once past the signal tower, the train accelerated as the wheels smoothly grooved on the straightaway toward the bridge. But at the same time when Train Number 3314 was whirring full speed ahead, it should have been preparing for a rapid deceleration and full stop.

The Newark Bay Bridge lift had gone up, tracks and all!

Nobody was more aware of the impending calamity than the skipper of a Newark Bay dredger, *Sand Captain*. Peder Pederson had been contracted to plow the sand off the Atlantic Ocean bottom and was piloting the 200-foot dredger out of the harbor towards Ambrose Lightship. He noted that the span had climbed into its open position and prepared to ease his shipwork through when he did a double-take. He detected the Jersey Central train hellbent for the bridge.

His warning alarm blaring across the bay, Pederson had his crew reverse engines. From his vantage point in the pilothouse, the skipper anxiously watched the five-car train as it irrevocably rolled toward its appointment with doom. The watch on Snuffy Stirnweiss' wrist indicated that it was almost 10 a.m.

A few passengers heard the alarm.

So did Tom Sellers, a youngster rowing with a friend in Newark Bay adjacent to the bridge. The 15-year-old could hear the loud report of the steel train on the steel bridge, followed by a dramatic change in sound as the last of the fail-safe devices went into play.

Train No. 3314 already had clattered past each of the three signal lights along the railroad approach to the bridge. As the train left the final red "Stop" light behind, the automatic derailer opened the track, sending the lead diesel engine's wheels off the steel track and onto the wooden crossties. According to an automatic tape retrieved from the locomotive, engineer Wilburn's train was careening across the span at a speed in excess of 35 miles per hour, and possibly as fast as 46 miles per hour. Although the derailer functioned according to its design, the momentum of the train carried it across the thick planks to the abyss.

The abyss at the railroad bridge where New York Yankees infielder George (Snuffy) Stirnweiss perished in 35 foot deep water.

– Stan Fischler Collection

Watching in horror, Captain Pederson neverthless could consider himself fortunate. His alarm failed to alert the train crew, but his swift action in reversing the *Sand Captain's* engines at full speed had removed the vessel from the locomotive's path.

The 6,000-foot run from the signal to the lip of lift bridge was complete. As passengers shrieked and gaped in panic, the diesel reached the open draw, leaped over the curved line of wood pilings and plunged to the waters 40 feet below. Engineer Wilburn's cap disappeared into Newark Bay, taking with it the second diesel locomotive, the first and second passenger coaches and half of the third coach, as the filthy water frothed with steam.

Several survivors, later taken to Bayonne (New Jersey) General Hospital, told reporters that they sensed disaster the moment the automatic derailing device sent the locomotive careening along the wooden ties. "I wondered if the bridge would close in time and the boat would crack up or whether the bridge would stay up and we would go down," said one rider who had detected the open bridge before others.

Another commuter remembered that some passengers had panicked while others had tried to calm them or shouted to them to be quiet. A regular Jersey Central passenger, Paul V. Land, who had been riding the same train for 15 years, recalled his anxiety over the train's speed. "The engineer was going like the devil," he said. "But I like to travel fast and I wasn't even looking out the window. Suddenly the brakes were applied and I thought: 'We're off the track.' I could hear ties being smashed by the train for maybe 1,000 feet. Then the trestle behind us disappeared.

"Then I was underwater. I thought: 'Thank God I have lots of insurance.' Then I remember my wallet floating. I grabbed it and put it into my pocket. I don't know why I grabbed the wallet. There was only $10 in it. I thought I was finished. I can't see how I survived."

Passenger Robert M. Klein described the episode as "fantastic." He had just closed his New Jersey summer home and was returning to Manhattan to rejoin his family. "As we got to the drawbridge I saw a medium-sized boat approaching. The train was moving fast.

"I thought: 'Either the boat makes it or we do.' I'm not too sure of what happened next. The brakes were jammed on, the train skidded. Then I found myself in the water. I was trapped under water. I thought I was drowned. I kept swimming upward. Suddenly I felt a surge of air. I pulled myself up out of the water and there was a boat."

At least one passenger had enough foresight to not only sense the impending disaster, but make preparations for his escape. Lloyd Nelson, who had been a passenger on *The Broker*, which had crashed in Woodbridge, New Jersey, in 1951, realized that the open drawbridge might not close in time. Nelson promptly opened the window next to his seat (cars on the Jersey Central were of such vintage that windows regularly could be opened and closed) and awaited the fateful plunge. "By the time the car was in the water," said Nelson, "I had the window open all the way. I swam to the surface and grabbed a hunk of piling that must have been knocked loose by the train. I floated on it for about 300 yards until I was picked up."

Another veteran of the Broker-Woodbridge disaster, Gustave H. Planitz, had only recently recovered from the previous train wreck, when he had been thrown into Newark Bay. He managed to swim to safety.

Onlookers rushed to rescue the survivors. Their hopes rested on the possibility that some passengers and crew, sensing the tragedy, might have leaped clear or that others, somehow, would find openings that would enable them to swim to safety.

Tom Sellers, the teenager who had been rowing in the bay, recovered from the shock of witnessing the wreck and rowed as mightily as he could to a woman floundering in the waves. Extending the oar from his rowboat, Sellers pulled her to safety.

Meanwhile, rescuers from the *Sand Captain* and from pleasure boats at a nearby marina rushed to the scene. They were greeted by the sight of half a passenger car hanging against the concrete-and-steel bridge superstructure. They groped for signs of life — and found them.

One passenger was in the middle of the third car, hanging precariously from the tracks above.

A tugboat moves in while a helicopter hovers over the open draw bridge at the scene of the Jersey Central wreck near Bayonne.
– Stan Fischler Collection

111

Crawling along the baggage rack, he managed to reach the upper dry area and clambered out into broad daylight.

By now emergency alarms had been radioed to Jersey Central officials, the police, firemen, and the Coast Guard. All forms of rescue vehicles were dispatched to the scene.

They arrived too late to change the course of the calamity. Those in the water who were able to swim clear were picked up by nearby vessels. Those in the two rear coaches, traumatized by the bouncing, were taken to safety.

Everyone in the first four pieces of rolling stock, from engineer Wilburn's locomotive through the second passenger coach, was doomed. Forty-eight persons died at the moment of the crash into Newark Bay or were drowned in the aftermath.

The deaths of Wilburn and fireman Andrew severely complicated investigation of the mysterious plunge of Train No. 3314. Nevertheless, the railroad and three governmental agencies — the Army Corps of Engineers, the New Jersey Public Utilities Commission and the Interstate Commerce Commission — each began a seperate inquiry into the disaster.

One of the few tangible clues was the locomotive tape which recorded the speed of the commuter train. Analysts were astonished to learn that the train actually *had slowed down* at the first bridge warning signal, but then had resumed speed until it was travelling well in excess of 40 miles per hour as it reached the lip of the span.

It was incomprehensible that either Wilburn or Andrew would deliberately run three signals and allow their train to dive into Newark Bay. It was equally difficult to imagine that either fireman or engineer would fail to activate braking systems once they were confronted with amber and red danger signals.

Examination of the crew's medical history disclosed that the fireman had been ordered on restricted duty because of his blood pressure and that the engineer's blood pressure had been on a steady, if not ominous, climb. Probers therefore focused their attention on the medical examinations for further clues.

Following a period of confusion over the preliminary autopsy, a more complete examination of the bodies of the engineer and fireman was conducted by the Hudson (New Jersey) County medical examiner's office. Three weeks after the disaster the final autopsy report was released by Dr. Angelo Gnassi, Hudson County's chief pathologist. According to Dr. Gnassi, Wilburn, the engineer, died of drowning. Fireman Andrew, while the victim of multiple fractures and bruises, had died, the autopsy revealed, at some point *before* the train had left the tracks.

Since there were no witnesses inside the locomotive cab, apart from Wilburn and Andrew, investigators were forced to rely on the locomotive's speed tape and on other bits and pieces of evidence collected along the track and in the waters of Newark Bay. Then, piecing the parts together, they hoped to come to a conclusion about the mysterious crash.

Examination of the rolling stock revealed that the air brakes on Train No. 3314 were in working order the day of the doomed ride. Further, it was determined that all warning signals on the approach to the lift had been in a normal working condition. When engineer Wilburn's locomotive has hauled out of Newark Bay, investigators examined its throttle and brake mechanism and deduced that the brakes had not been applied until the diesel was within a few yards of the open span. The throttle, while not in the closed position, was, in fact, in the next notch, which would only allow the train to crawl, at best.

With Holmesian logic, the investigators ultimately concluded that the tragedy was triggered by not one but two physical aberrations inside the cab of the lead diesel, one affecting the engineer, the other victimizing his fireman.

Consequent to the disaster, the New Jersey Public Utilities Commission made the dead-man switch mandatory on all passenger railroads within the state. But by that time it was too late to save the life of Snuffy Stirnweiss and the 47 other victims of the Jersey Central's ill-fated commuter train.

Hanging limply, the forlorn coach is about to be deposited on a waiting barge.
– Stan Fischler Collection

During the steam era the Rolls Royce of Long Island Rail Road locomotives was the G-5 built by the parent Pennsylvania Railroad in its Juniata shops. G-5 is seen here near Mill Neck Station on the Oyster Bay Branch in 1953. — Stan Fischler Collection

SECTION IV — ANATOMY OF A NETWORK

CHAPTER 15: REACHING INTO THE NEW ERA

If one could pinpoint a "Golden Age" of commuter railroading in the New York metropolitan area it would be the years 1890-1950. Henry Ford's horseless carriage was not yet ready to challenge the likes of the Jersey Central; Delaware, Lackawanna and Western; or, for that matter, the Long Island Rail Road. "Everywhere," noted John T. Cunningham, railroad historian, "the railroads gathered public favor. Accidents declined, service improved, comfort grew. Railroads made money and railroads spent money. Above all, the railroads apparently had well in hand for all time the problem of getting from one place to another in a hurry."

No state in the Union offered more for commuters than New Jersey. It was a rare hamlet that was more than ten miles from a train station. Trips to New York City were frequent whether you rode the Lackawanna, Susquehanna, Erie or Central.

In 1892 a Jersey Central locomotive (Baldwin-built) steamed two miles in 75 seconds, a world's record speed of 105 miles per hour. Competition among the various lines bred excellence, including along routes which had been notorious for poor safety records. Even the Erie, regarded as the clown prince of Eastern railroads late in the 19th century, began to shape up in 1901 under the vibrant leadership of Fred Underwood. Anyone courageous enough to take over the Erie's helm had to be equipped with a sense of humor, and Underwood was. When asked why he carried an ax with him in his private car, he explained, "That is in case we have an accident and I have to chop my way out!"

But Underwood was serious about improving the Erie. In no time at all workmen were on the tracks easing curves, lessening grades and, on a more personal basis, improving service. The improvements didn't change the Erie's image overnight. It remained the butt of humorists, much in the manner that the Long Island Rail Road does today.

Rather than rail over the slings and arrows hurled by critics, Underwood jumped on the laugh bandwagon. He told friends that "if it weren't for the Erie half the vaudeville performers would be looking for jobs."

When the Erie issued its 1906 timetable, Underwood made sure that it contained a quip about his railroad. "Spring is here at last," started one of the gags, "the Erie has replaced the snowplows on its cow-catchers with mowing machines."

Another timetable offered this bit of humor: "A commuter suggested that the Erie put a cow-catcher on the rear of the train. No Erie train is liable to overtake a cow, but what's to prevent a cow from walking on the back of a car and biting a passenger?" Underwood amassed a large collection of these Erie gags and made a book out of them.

Underwood also employed his acute sense of public relations to advantage. He placed the names of outstanding engineers on the sides of new locomotives rolling onto the Erie's tracks. Other competent engineers were honored by having an "Order Of The Red Spot" (a bright carmine disk) placed under the engine's number plate.

Taking its cue from the Erie, the New York, Susquehanna and Western honored its favorite engineer, Philip T. Nixon, by naming engine Number 12 after him. Nixon, who never swore, drank or smoked, was devoted to the Methodist Episcopal Church, whose services he helped bring to Hawthorne, New Jersey, in 1893. He also helped raise funds to complete erection of a railroad station in the town. Nixon also is remembered for the patience displayed when his name was misspelled on the engine plate. Instead of Philip, the plate read Phillip. Nixon laughed it off. Not until some 4,000 miles later, when the engine was ready for an overhaul, was the extra *l* dropped from the name plate.

The public of the day professed affection for the commuter rail lines and their employees. Broadway reflected the influence of the railroad. The theater featured such railroad-oriented plays as *The Midnight Special, Railroad Jack* and *The Pay Train*.

Occasionally, commuters themselves got into the headlines with acts of heroism. One such individual was a Miss Nellie Hand, who discovered wood from a blown-down shed lying across the Reading Railroad tracks one dark night.

She found a usable lantern at a railroad crossing and sprinted up the tracks in the direction of an oncoming New York-bound train. Waving the danger signal as vigorously as possible, Miss Hand caught the engineer's attention and he applied the brakes in time to avert disaster. Before the trainmen could alight to thank her, Nellie walked home, secure in a job well done. But the railroaders weren't satisfied and made a determined effort to locate the heroine. Within a week, Nellie was identified as the person who had saved the Reading from a crash and was offered a suitable reward. "No thanks," she replied, "anyone would have done the same thing if they were in my shoes."

At least one line — the Morris and Essex Division of the Lackawanna — refused to run trains on Sunday. Wags suggested that M&E stood not for Morris and Essex, but for Methodist & Episcopal. But by the turn of the century, the Lackawanna had become progressive enough to lift its ban on Sunday trains and it launched a series of excursion runs to such popular resorts as Lake Hopatcong and the Delaware Water Gap.

Lake Hopatcong was also a favorite depot for the Jersey Central, which deposited thousands of happy excursionists at Nolan's Point. In the early part of the 20th century, it was not uncommon for the Central to haul 60,000 passengers each Summer to Nolan's Point, where city dwellers enjoyed a dance pavilion, swings, walking path, excursion grounds and, of course, the magnificent lake itself. Gustave Kobbe, in his book about the Jersey Central, noted that many commuters "concentrated a whole year's holiday into one day at the lake." He added, "There is almost a touch of pathos in their unbounded delight."

On the other side of the Hudson, the Long Island Rail Road also was busily developing its links with resorts. The Rockaway Beach division of the LIRR was electrified in 1905 and became one of the most popular runs on the railroad. Five years later the Long Island electrified its branch to Long Beach, another popular resort on the Atlantic Ocean. To reach the Rockaways, the LIRR trains plied a lengthy wooden trestle over Jamaica Bay. Frequent fires were the bane of the Jamaica Bay trestle, and cold winters produced ice floes. Frequently the floes, ramming against the trestle superstructure, would knock it out of alignment, necessitating repairs and delays.

Exploiting the amusement areas was one source of revenue for the commuter lines, but the meat and potatoes was still provided by the Monday-to-Friday operation. The New York and Long Branch (New Jersey) line, jointly operated by the Pennsylvania and Jersey Central railroads, was originally developed for resort business. But by the early 1900's this, too, had became a major source of passenger revenue as a weekday commuter service.

Red Bank, for example, once regarded as a resort, blossomed into a residential community largely populated with homeowners who worked in Manhattan. The New York and Long Branch was their vehicle for survival. Likewise, wealthy businessmen who established residency around Freehold, in the Colt's Neck area, as well as Rumson-Fair Haven, relied on the New York and Long Branch. "Private subscription club cars were the order of the day for commuting," wrote Lawrence Grow in *On the 8:02*.

Through the 1920's more and more bulding lots sprouted along the Jersey shore, and consequently more people rode the New York and Long Branch. And similar growth was evident in other parts of New Jersey.

The Lackawanna, for instance, benefited from development of land west of the Oranges. Communities such as Morristown, Dover, Montclair and Chatham became havens for the middle class, upper middle class, and even those from the highest social stratum. In a 1901 report in the *The New York Daily Tribune* about life in surburbia, the writer commented on the psyche of the commuter as follows:

"He calls his Jersey home his country place, speaks of it as a sort of paradise on earth, and commiserates a chap for having to live in an apartment or flat in the city."

Lackawanna passenger ridership spiraled upward following construction of a double-track 4,283-foot tunnel under Jersey City in 1877, which provided a through route to the waterfront for passenger and freight trains. Heretofore, passenger trains had been operating to Jersey City via the Bergen Tunnel route of the Erie Railroad. But the Lackawanna needed its own depot on the Hudson River and a vast new ferry-passenger terminal building finally was completed in the latter part of the 19th century. In August 1905, when fire levelled the structure, the DL&W promptly constructed a new facility with a two-level concourse, ferry slips and a 14-track train shed covering 4.79 acres. The new terminal was opened in February 1907 and soon was complemented by a second double-track tunnel under Jersey City, completed in 1908. The Hoboken Terminal of the Lackawanna proved a bustling operation. In 1914 total traffic there required the three interlocking plants (which controlled train movements) to make 28,721,700 switch and signal movements regulating them.

Nearby, along the Hudson waterfront, the Erie also was busily improving its operations in the early 1900's. The passenger terminal, situated between the Erie's north and south freight yards in Jersey City, was extensively modernized in 1910-1911. This was to accomodate increased ridership which, in turn, was due to the opening of new all-passenger routes through New Jersey in 1910. New electric-pneumatic interlocking towers were erected at Grove Street and at a point just west of an enlarged 11-track train shed and terminal. "A typical weekday operation," wrote William H. Sheppard in *Tidewater Terminals of the Erie Lackawanna Railway*, "in 1913 saw 76,500 passengers handled by 538 train movements requiring 9,732 lever movements at Terminal Tower alone!"

The Erie's waterfront facilities at Weehawken adjoined those of the Central Railroad of New Jersey and of the New York Central's West Shore division. Each depot reflected the prosperity of commuter railroading in the early 1900's.

Development also came to New York Central territory throughout suburban Westchester County. The affluent middle class began deserting the city for more spacious acreage in Scarsdale, White Plains, Chappaqua and Mamaroneck. "Pleasure spots for the day or weekend excursion," commented Lawrence Grow, "opened up by the railroad became, in time, residential suburban territory. Railroad executives encouraged settlement by *first* building seasonal facilities such as hotels and picnic grounds. Permanent residents were soon to follow."

The New York Central touted communities on its Harlem Division whenever possible. The village of Bedford, for example, was hailed by the Central as a place where "rare combinations of mountain, stream, and foliage greet the eye in endless variety, the whole forming a panorama of rural scenery incomparable for beauty, picturesqueness and variety."

When the Central electrified its commuter line between Grand Central Station and North White Plains in 1910 it offered still more stimuli for New Yorkers contemplating a move to Westchester. Soon trains were running from Grand Central to White Plains.

Communities along the Hudson — Riverdale (The Bronx), Yonkers, Tarrytown, Ardsley and Irvington, to name a few — were on the Central's Hudson Division, but development there was slower than for the communities on the Harlem Division. Still, the Central encouraged growth by

An ancient LIRR steam engine chugs onto the turntable en route to the shops.
– Stan Fischler Collection

electrifying the Hudson Division as far as the town of Croton-on-Hudson in 1913. Passenger traffic described a continuous increase on that branch well into the 1920's.

Least successful of the New York Central's commuter operations was the Putnam Division, described as "a railroad that no one really wanted for many years." It ran northeasterly from Yonkers through Westchester and Putnam counties on a general line about midway between its Harlem and Hudson Division cousins, serving such towns as Yonkers, Pocantico Hills and Yorktown Heights. In 1926 the Putnam Division was electrified too, but it never attained the ridership of either the Hudson or Harlem divisions.

Easily the most curious of the developing commuter lines operated by the Central in the 1900's was the West Shore Railroad, which the Central obtained in 1885 as the New York, West Shore and Buffalo Railway.

Unlike the other New York Central commuter lines which originated at Grand Central Terminal in Manhattan, the West Shore Division's depot was located across the Hudson River in Weehawken, New Jersey. A ferry service then carried passengers across to New York. The West Shore Division rolled northward from Weehawken through such affluent Jersey hamlets as Little Ferry, Ridgefield Park and Teaneck, eventually crossing the state line into Rockland County, New York, and towns such as West Nyack, Valley Cottage, Congers and West Haverstraw. While most of the runs terminated at West Haverstraw, the West Shore occasionally dispatched trains through to Newburgh and Cornwall-on-the-Hudson. In addition to ridership generated by commuter traffic, the West Shore Division also benefited from excursion business to popular Bear Mountain resort, as well as to the United States Military Academy at West Point.

"As was the case on the other side of the Hudson in the 1890's," said Lawrence Grow, "and the early decades of the 20th century, farmland slowly gave way to residential development, old Dutch barns to solid middle-class cottages."

The numbers of middle-class homes multiplied and, since there still was no such thing as a George Washington Bridge or Lincoln Tunnel, the West Shore Railroad was *the* way to get to Bergen County, New Jersey, and Rockland County, New York.

A distant cousin of the New York Central's West Shore Railroad was the New York, New Haven and Hartford, if only because it operated out of the Central's palatial depot in Manhattan, Grand Central Terminal. Like the Central, the New Haven made a great leap forward by electrifying its main line from Woodlawn, New York, to Stamford, Connecticut. In 1907 the first regular New Haven train to run behind electric power rolled out of Grand Central. The 21-mile electrification proved a boon to commuters, since it covered such burgeoning suburban centers as Mount Vernon, New Rochelle, Harrison, Rye, Port Chester and Cos Cob.

The New Haven was in the right place at the right time, and ridership figures proved it; between 1900 and 1910 commuter business in and out of Grand Central almost doubled, and it more than doubled in the decade following. Aware of the high-class calibre of their clientele, New Haven executives ordered a number of amenities for the Westchester-Connecticut commuters.

"The trips," wrote Lawrence Grow, "were made as comfortable as possible for these busy executives; even the conductors were noted for their clubby good cheer. F.A. Shute was one such friendly presence on the New Canaan Express each day. From the early 1900's until 1935, he ministered to the needs of his charges. Unbeknownst to them, he also studied the manners and mores of the one thousand daily riders . . . The conductor had his own way of sizing up a new recruit, to measure how well he would fit the local commuter mold:

"If he reached the station on time and in good humor; if he could manage a newspaper without getting it all mussed up and without too much waving of the arms in the process; if he refrained from talking to his fellow passengers when they were reading, working, or trying to sleep; if he could find his ticket without hunting through all his pockets; if he could sleep sitting upright and awake automatically just before reaching his destination; if he was perfectly shameless about the parcels he carried, feeling free to come into the train with a lawn mower, a watermelon, a scythe, an armful of roses or a statue of Winged Victory, I'd say to myself, 'He'll do'."

Nobody, in the "Golden Era" could question the fact that the New Haven was doing its job well. The same could be said for the Long Island Rail Road, although in 1900 the LIRR had to be saved from bankruptcy by the Pennsylvania Railroad. When Pennsylvania Station was completed in midtown Manhattan and tunnels burrowed under the East River linking the LIRR with Penn Station, the Long Island began enjoying the kind of prosperity that encouraged the New Haven and the New York Central to increase their commuter operations. The LIRR management vigorously pursued every avenue in wooing potential riders to its trains. One obvious strategy was to lure New Yorkers into settling on Long Island.

"Why not know this friendly, charming place of great lawns, deep verandas, and country

clubs brilliant and simple; of harbors and inlets that are a joy forever of yachtsmen; of model farms, oyster beds, and aeroplane schools; of Elizabethan cottages and French chateaux; of magical agricultural experiments under the wisdom of a great railroad whose story is the modern story of Long Island; of white beaches which sometimes, it is rumored, end in lovers' meetings, and of the old, old sea?

"Why not know Long Island and real life?"

It was a pitch many accepted. The LIRR, already doing good business at the turn of the century, solidified its reputation as the greatest commuter line in the United States, with the most involved labyrinth of suburban routes along the Eastern Seaboard. Growth on the LIRR followed the pattern evident with the New Haven and New York Central.

Panoramic view of the Long Island Rail Road's Jamaica Station in 1904 shows, at right, one of the railroad's 500-series locomotives, heading east towards the old, ground-level station. Locomotive #512 was among the few highest-numbered engines the LIRR had, and came to the railroad following consolidation with other railroads. This photograph was taken

Electrification was the key. With a total of 38 route miles for starters, the Long Island was electrified from Flatbush Avenue Terminal in Brooklyn, east to Belmont Park. The electrification continued south from Woodhaven Junction across Jamaica Bay, to Rockaway Park and Valley Stream via Far Rockaway. Electrification was also extended to Hempstead and Mineola in 1908, and in 1910 the Long Island trains were welcomed, via the East River tunnels, into Penn Station. This great leap forward was followed by electrification of the North Shore Division.

Modernization of the Long Island was translated into new rolling stock in 1905 and 1906, when 134 steel multiple unit cars — designed by railroad consultant George Gibbs and known as "Gibbs Cars" — were built for the electrified Long Island. Considerably less imposing than the electric multiple unit cars which ran on the New Haven, the LIRR rolling stock was strikingly

from approximately 147th Street, Jamaica, looking east towards the station. The massive grade crossing elimination and raising of all station and switching facilities, (above) began a short time after. The work was completed in 1913.
— photo courtesy of Long Island-Sunrise Trail Chapter, National Railway Historical Society

similar to the new trains which had just begun operating on the New York City Interborough Rapid Transit (IRT) subway.

There was a method to this. City planners hoped to link the LIRR trains coming in to Atlantic Avenue with the IRT tracks and have the Long Island trains ply city routes as well. However, the plan never reached fruition.

A second set of new cars was put into operation soon after 1910. Featuring circular windows, which gave the appearance of a pair of giant eyes, the rolling stock was distinctly different from the original Gibbs cars that so closely simulated the IRT subway trains. The new cars, inspired by Pennsylvania Railroad blueprints, were 13 feet longer than the Gibbs vehicles (which measured 51 feet) and weighed 54 tons, more than 13 tons heavier. Labelled Class MP54, the new rolling stock became the trademark of the LIRR and within five years of delivery were rolling over 89 route miles and 188 track miles of main line now electrified. With the financial assistance of the Pennsy, the Long Island continued to improve, eliminating dangerous grade crossings, constructing new stations and further electrifying the line whenever possible.

The results were more than gratifying to the parent Pennsy. Ridership went up and operating costs went down. From 1905, when the Long Island's first electric train began rolling, through 1919, the railroad boasted a 353 percent gain in passenger ticket sales!

The upward spiral continued through the early 1920's and more cars, similar to the popular and efficient MP54's, were added, until the fleet numbered almost 1,000 electric passenger cars. As the 1930's approached, the Long Island had clearly established itself as the number one commuter line in North America. More than 60 percent of the railroad commuters in the United States rode what had become known during the 1920's as "The Route Of The Dashing Commuters."

As along the Long Island's routes, a pattern of development was evident along the diverse suburban network of the Erie Railroad. Unlike the LIRR, the Erie's growth was stimulated more by the acquisition of a number of local or regional companies than anything else. The Erie's Jersey City Terminal became thronged with passengers travelling to and from towns such as Hackensack, Montclair, Elizabeth, Rutherfurd (now Rutherford) and Godwinville (now Ridgewood). In many ways the Erie's development as a commuter line paralleled that of the nearby Delaware, Lackawanna and Western, which much later merged with the Erie, thereby producing the Erie-Lackawanna.

An Erie Lackawanna oldtimer sits in the yards.
– Stan Fischler Collection

Islip Station, in 1911, looked like this, with Long Island Rail Road locomotive #223 waiting for its departure time. A horse, with buggy, stands serenely to the side. This locomotive, a D-16, was one of the most successful American built engines and 430 of them were constructed by the Pennsylvania Railroad between 1895 and 1910 – ten came to the LIRR; another 21 were added in 1906. Most of the locomotives were retired in the Twenties. Islip Station was razed and replaced in 1963. It had been built in 1868 by the South Side Railroad, and came under LIRR jurisdiction when the South Side and the North Side railroads consolidated with the LIRR. Long Island-Sunrise Trail Chapter, National Railway Historical Society

In at least one case, that of the village of Montclair, New Jersey, both the Erie and Lackawanna offered service and separate depots. The Erie also linked Jersey City (and New York City via the Erie ferry) with such blossoming communities as Tenafly, Englewood, Leonia and Oradell, New Jersey, as well as Nyack and Spring Valley, in Rockland County, New York.

Like the Lackawanna, the Erie also headed south through New Jersey and, according to some experts, performed more nobly than its competitor. "The Orange branch of the Erie," commented Lawrence Grow, "was quite a fancy affair in the early days and offered the commuter much better service than that available on the Lackawanna. The West Orange station featured walnut-panelled waiting rooms with fireplaces." Equally impressive were the Erie stations in ritzy Tuxedo (as in Tuxedo Junction) and Harriman on the route that took the trains all the way to the Erie's tri-state (New York-New Jersey-Pennsylvania) terminus at Port Jervis, N.Y. But the Erie never electrified in the manner of the Lackawanna or Long Island, so it never quite achieved their eminence as a commuter carrier.

By contrast, the Pennsyvania, despite its accent on long-range passenger service, did a hefty commuter business between New York City and Trenton, New Jersey. Between those stations, the Pennsy commuter locals stopped at Elizabeth, Rahway, Metuchen, New Brunswick and Princeton.

Coincident with the sprouting of railroad lines was an equally vigorous proliferation of electric street railways on Long Island, in Westchester and Connecticut and throughout northern and central New Jersey. Many of these high-speed trolleys (also known as interurbans) linked directly with the railways and proved to be excellent commuter carriers. In New Jersey, for example, a commuter starting a trip in Jersey City could, in the years 1910-1920, connect by interurban with such diverse locales as Wharton, Dover, Denville, Boonton, Morris Plains, Caldwell, Coytesville and even Suffern, across the state line, in New York.

The "Golden Age" of commuter railroading changed the face of suburbia. Meadowlands gave way to housing sub-divisions. Dairy farms turned into middle-class developments and such expressions as "Change at Jamaica" — the bane of every Long Island rider — became part of the American lexicon.

The suburbanite, himself, was epitomized by the white Anglo-Saxon, upper-middle-class businessman who cherished his residence's distance from the madness of Manhattan. The commuter railroads made possible a physical and social distance between him and the refugee hordes in The Gotham. Nobody expressed this sentiment better than a chap named Gustav Kobbe, a drumbeater for the Jersey Central when that railroad was rapidly developing a high-class commuter clientele.

"It may be said that thousands of the best citizens of New York are not citizens of that city at all. In the morning they flood the business districts of the metropolis; in the evening they ebb away. They are citizens of New York in so far as the city owes to their brains and energy a great share of its prosperity; they are not citizens in that they live and vote elsewhere. If this great suburban army of intelligent men lived as well as worked in New York, we would probably hear less of the necessity of municipal reform, for there would be just so much more intelligence among the voting population — which brings us back to our starting point: that of New York's best citizens thousands are, unfortunately for it, citizens of suburbia."

CHAPTER 16:
THE DECLINE AND FALL OF PRACTICALLY EVERYBODY

There are those who believe that the end of the commuter railroads' "Golden Era" and the eventual decline and fall of practically every line in the New York metropolitan area are inevitable. Widespread use of the automobile, coupled with construction of the George Washington Bridge, the Lincoln Tunnel and a web of new highways ended the predominance of the rails as the primary means getting from Manhattan to suburbia and exurbia.

Yet there are a number of transit pundits who argue that the commuter lines weren't necessarily doomed to extinction or, as the case may be, limited operation. These critics maintain that the railroads were forced into such a position by the myopia of railroad barons and the politics of contemporary transit planners who accented rubber — as in cars and buses — over rails.

There is something to be said for both arguments, but evidence suggests that an attempt was made to kill the commuter lines through promulgation of policies that were unnecessary and unwarranted.

The downward turn began in the 1920's as the automobile proliferated, continued into the 1930's at a time when the motor bus began intruding on commuter railroad turf and — after a brief respite during World War II — the negative spiral resumed following the war.

Each line was affected in a different way. The New York Central, for example, saw its profits begin to dwindle following the great stock market crash of 1929.

The Depression of the 1930's did nothing to alleviate conditions and each of the Central's commuter divisions — the Hudson, Harlem, Putnam and West Shore — suffered. The Harlem, whose communities had developed more rapidly than any other suburbs in the New York metropolitan area, remained in business but service declined. When in the 1960's the New York Central and Pennsylvania Railroads merged to form the Penn Central, there was hope for improvement, but the new company suffered as many problems as its predecessors. Ultimately the Harlem Division was left to the mercy of the New York State Metropolitan Transportation Authority (MTA) and Conrail, governmental agencies which annexed the commuter lines.

The Hudson Division had the benefit of sharing trackage with the New York Central's — later Penn Central's — main line. It was consequently at some advantage through the 1970's, and improvements were gradually instituted to accomodate increased passenger service on the New York-Albany corridor.

The Putnam Division was less fortunate. Less securely established than its cousins, the Putnam lost ground with construction of the Saw Mill River Parkway before World War II. The line survived the war, but couldn't survive the 1950's. It fell victim to the cost-cutting policies of New York Central boss Alfred Perlman. In the 1930's the West Shore Railroad still operated eight morning and seven evening rush hour trains. But the hopes of a bright post-war future evaporated with construction of the New York State Thruway and Tappan Zee Bridge. The line was eventually

125

A bucolic scene along the Long Island Railroad. – courtesy John Krause

With the Hudson River on the left, a New York Central steamer heads towards Harmon, N.Y.
– courtesy Robert F. Collins

discontinued. A spate of critics, including Lawrence Grow, continued in their belief that the West Shore Division was prematurely put out of business and could, in fact, have remained operable and relatively successful to the present. "While the automobile may be blamed for the demise of the railroad, there is no evidence that the New York Central effectively utilized the suburban line or defended it against the encroachments of the internal combustion engine," wrote Grow, who also opined that the railroad could have continued service successfully as an alternative to the traffic jams now endemic to the area.

The decline and fall of the New York Central was a shocking reversal to railroad fans. The demise of the New Haven system was no less traumatic. The New Haven took a financial bath in its takeover of the New York, Westchester, and Boston Railroad. The line gambled on expansion of interurban trolley lines, only to discover that the public no longer flocked to the high-speed electric cars. Losses from these and other miscalculations piled up, and in 1935 a near-bankrupt New Haven was taken over by trustees. It continued in this dubious economic state until after World War II. Wartime restrictions against auto use helped, but only temporarily. Service continued to decline in the 1950's and 1960's. In 1961 the New Haven was bankrupt.

Just when it appeared that the New Haven would be counted out, Conrail, a federal government-operated rail corporation, in this instance supported by the states of New York and Connecticut, came to the rescue. A plan for long-range improvement was developed and put into implementation, on the theory that the maintenance of effective commuter railroads was essential to the welfare of both states.

In the long run electrification, for all its benefits, could save neither the New Haven nor the Long Island Rail Road. The LIRR continued to run trains out of its terminals in Brooklyn and Manhattan beyond the Depression years, but service in the immediate post-World War II era ranged from bad to worse and the result was an appalling drop in rail commuters. Many LIRR regulars switched to the automobile, utilizing the newly-constructed Long Island Expressway, then less tie-up prone than it is today. Rather than let the Long Island go the way of other defunct railroads, New York State assumed control of the faltering line, which became wholly owned by the (N.Y.) Metropolitan Transportation Authority (MTA).

Under the MTA banner, the LIRR began to see some improvement. Delivery of 620 new electric, multiple-unit cars manufactured by the Budd Company proved to be both anaesthetic and efficient shot in the arm, although the rolling stock suffered from gremlins in their early years. Slowly but surely, the Long Island won back riders who had abandoned it for the highways. Ironically, one positive factor was the Long Island highway system, which proved inadequate to handle the overwhelming numbers of commuter cars in the 1960's and 1970's.

In New Jersey there was some parallel with Long Island. The Delaware, Lackawanna and Western Railroad opted for electrification of its Morris and Essex Division as far west as Dover, in the late 1920's, as well as of its branch lines linking Newark with Montclair and from Summit to Gladstone. In anticipation of the modernized service, the DL&W ordered 141 pieces of new rolling stock from Pullman. These cars seated 84 passengers and began operations in 1929. Just two years later electrification of the entire network of DL&W commuter lines was complete. Riders were pleased. The new cars were not only attractive for their time, but quiet, speedy and generally efficient. "Running times," commented William D. Middleton in his book *When the Steam Railroads Electrified*, "were reduced by an average of 25 per cent, and trains were operated much more frequently." Traffic through the Hoboken terminal steadily increased to over 300 persons per minute during rush-hour periods and, despite the Depression, the DL&W commuter lines stayed in business.

The Erie, which never electrified, began accenting freight service over passenger business. By 1956 the Jersey City depot of the Erie had been shuttered and remaining trains moved to the Hoboken station of the DL&W. A merger between the Erie and Lackawanna seemed inevitable, and in 1960 it finally happened, producing the Erie-Lackawanna.

Pulling the classic Stilwell cars, Erie #2512 heads for Port Jervis, N.Y.
– courtesy of John Krause

Erie-Lackawanna at Dover. — courtesy John Krause

With the Hudson River as a backdrop, a Croton-bound commuter train races northward.
— Stan Fischler Collection

The Central Railroad of New Jersey presents another but not dissimilar story. In its heyday the Jersey Central had spread across the length and breadth of New Jersey. It reached coastal resorts as well as inland communities and provided a service which survived on local freight and passenger revenue. Like its cousin railroads on both sides of the Hudson, the Jersey Central exploited the fact that the communities it served had become the bedroom towns for New York City.

Unfortunatley for CNJ, coal-hauling comprised the backbone of its business. Early in the 20th century, coal revenues were sufficient to keep the railroad on track financially, but with the approach of the 1940's, the national economic structure had sufficiently changed to adversely affect CNJ. "The financial weakness of CNJ was inherent," wrote Peter Rickerhauser in *Trains* magazine, "because the pressures of the 20th century eventually affected a railroad based on the economic realities of the 19th century." The CNJ went bankrupt in 1939. It was reorganized but suffered a second bankruptcy in 1949. At the time of the Newark Bay Bridge commuter train disaster in 1958, the Jersey Central contemplated still another bankruptcy proceeding. It was a difficult time, and any hope for salvation could only be provided by the state government. Finally in 1964 the State of New Jersey began subsidizing commuter service. Two years later it changed the onerous tax requirements of the railroad to lessen the heavy financial burden the carrier bore.

By the Spring of 1965 the commuter railroad situation in the New York metropolitan area was in a critical state.

In April 1965 it was revealed that two of the CNJ's five Hudson River ferries — the Red Bank and Somerville — had to be removed from service because they could not meet U.S. Coast Guard safety standards and the cost of rehabilitating them was beyond the railroad's ability. Compensating for the loss, Jersey Central made arrangements with New York City to lease two radar- and radio-equipped diesel-electric ferryboats, the *Tides* and the *Narrows*, which previously had been used on the 69th Street (Brooklyn)-Staten Island run.

Meanwhile, the Erie-Lackawanna announced it would be forced to abandon its New Jersey commuter railroad services unless the State of New Jersey developed a "concrete plan" to defray all losses and provide funds for modernization within three to five months (which would have placed it at the Fall-Winter of 1965). William White, chairman of the Erie-Lackawanna, stated that the railroad was not giving the state an ultimatum, but that the company was no longer able to bear huge losses (despite state subsidy of the commuter service) or meet the cost of equipment replacement needed to continue the service. Reinforcing White's position was a financial analysis of the commuter service prepared by Wyer, Dick and Company, Transportation Consultants of Upper Montclair, New Jersey.

The consultants concluded that the New Jersey commuter lines were losing $7,205,624 each year and added that if deferred maintenance needs were met the loss would increase by $783,244 to $7,988,868. At the time the State of New Jersey's commuter subsidy to the Erie-Lackawanna was only about $2,200,000.

Curiously, the report revealed that the Erie-Lackawanna was actually making money when commuter subsidies were included with revenues on its two most heavily-used commuter lines: the diesel-operated Bergen County route to Suffern, New York, and the electrically-operated Morris and Essex Division services to Summit, Gladstone and Dover, New Jersey. However, those profits were offset by heavy losses on the light-density lines.

Using the report as the basis for his response, White outlined an $80,000,000 modernization program required to preserve the status quo for Erie-Lackawanna's commuter service. White also

A handsome diesel hums into Croton-Harmon Station. — Stan Fischler Collection

suggested that the State of New Jersey form an agency to rent the Erie-Lackawanna commuter service. He stated that the railroad would be willing to give such an agency its aging equipment in return for an agreement under which the state would absorb all costs of the servicer and the EL would receive an annual rental and management fee.

If the Erie-Lackawanna executives could take any solace in their misery, it was only because their colleagues running the New Haven Railroad were in an even worse pickle. By the Winter of 1964-65 the New Haven had petitioned the Interstate Commerce Commission for approval of a drastic reduction in its commuter service. The routes in question included those between Fairfield County, Connecticut, Westchester County, New York, and Grand Central Terminal. "The Larchmont Plan," as the New Haven's scheme was described, called for discontinuance of all service at the New Haven stations nearest to New York City — Mount Vernon, Columbus Avenue, Pelham and New Rochelle. Off-peak service at the ten suburban stations between Larchmont and Stamford would be substantially reduced.

Federal Judge Robert P. Anderson, whose District Court in New Haven was responsible for the bankrupt New Haven line, denounced the two states (New York and Connecticut) served by the railroad for failing to subsidize passenger services.

It was determined that if the Larchmont Plan took effect it would deny service to about 7,500 of the New Haven's 25,000 New York-area commuters. The New Haven's proposals evoked a strong response from the state governments in Albany and Hartford. Governor Nelson A. Rockefeller of New York and his Connecticut counterpart, John N. Dempsey, proposed the revival of an earlier plan to buy 80 new multiple-unit-type cars for the New Haven to replace its worn-out pre-World War II cars.

In what was to become a decision of far-reaching import, the governors also made it clear that

Approaching Croton-Harmon on a cold winter day. — Stan Fischler Collection

modernizing the New Haven commuter service was only a first step. They envisioned the line becoming a suburban rapid transit operation and followed up their plan by holding intensive consultations with the federal government on the idea.

Rockefeller meant business, and on February 25, 1965, he endorsed the proposal for creation of a New York State Metropolitan Commuter Transportation Authority which, among other things, would acquire and modernize the Long Island Rail Road, as well as purchase or lease the New Haven's facilities. The Rockefeller blueprints called for the integration of New Haven commuter service with that of the Hudson and Harlem divisions of the then New York Central. *Headlights* magazine, published by the Electric Railroaders' Association, commented, "The only choice for the commuter service into New York City lies between an indefinite subsidy of an inefficient railroad commuter service or its conversion into a suburban rapid transit operation."

The most optimistic proposals were those generated by Rockefeller for the LIRR. Endorsing a plan which called for public ownership of the Long Island, and conversion of much of it into a high-speed suburban rapid transit system, Rockefeller commissioned a blue ribbon committee to produce a plan of operation for the ailing line. The three major recommendations of the Special Committee were:

* Purchase of the LIRR by New York State from its sole owner, the Pennsylvania Railroad, if a reasonable price could be obtained. The railroad could neither survive nor obtain funds for needed modernization under private enterprise.

* Creation of a New York State Metropolitan Commuter Transportation Authority to assume responsibility for the operation of the Long Island. In the judgement of the Special Committee, this authority could also assume responsibility for other commuter activities throughout the New York State portion of the New York City metropolitan area.

* Completion by 1970 of a $200,000,000 modernization and rehabilitation of the Long Island, which would be undertaken by the New York State Metropolitan Commuter Transportation Authority.

Several benefits were projected if the Rockefeller proposal were adopted. These included the following:

* New York State would save millions of dollars from the modernization and rehabilitation of the LIRR compared with the enormous cost of highway construction required if the railroad were abandoned. The proposed Metropolitan Commuter Transportation Authority would give it a flexible operating agency to assure the continuation and improvement of other vital transportation services in the region.

* The communities served by the LIRR would not only gain continued operation of the railroad, but would have a vastly improved rapid transit service capable of accommodating a 25 percent increase in traffic, while giving passengers better and more comfortable service.

* The commuters would gain a modern, high-speed, comfortable and reliable service in an air-conditioned fleet.

The committee concluded that public ownership of the LIRR was the only practical way to assure its continued operation.

With creation of the state's Metropolitan Transportation Authority (MTA), Rockefeller's dream soon became a reality, and in 1965 the MTA took title to the railroad from the Pennsy. Rockefeller was determined to rejuvenate the Long Island into what he suggested would be "the best railroad in the country." The state pumped $360,000,000 into an overhaul of the system. Vital to the rehabilitation was the purchase of new rolling stock, which began in 1968. Other improvements in the physical plant, including tracks and signals, permanently changed the character of the LIRR. It began to operate like a working railroad again.

Thus, it became clear at the dawn of the 1970's that all was not lost on the New York commuter railroad front, although it would be impossible to resurrect lines such as the New York Central's West Shore Division, already scrapped. Thanks to Nelson Rockefeller and other politicians with foresight, the commuter lines entered the 1970's convinced that a better day lay ahead.

CHAPTER 17: RISING FROM THE ASHES

Pulling together the dilapidated fragments of the Westchester and Connecticut lines was no small task. Essentially, a public transportation network was pieced together out of the private lines which had suffered financial failures in the 20 years after World War II. Although public assistance began slowly, without forewarning of how extensive it would come to be, by the mid-1960's officials in New York, New Jersey, and Connecticut realized that it would that it would take far more than a dollop of dollars to set the commuter lines back on the right track.

First the Port Authority of New York and New Jersey was given legislative approval for a program of limited assistance. The Port Authority could purchase equipment and then lease it to the commuter lines, reducing their capital costs and spurring modernization. The New York Central was thus able to obtain 87 new electrified multiple-unit cars under this plan between 1962 and 1965, so that it could better operate its routes along the Hudson River's east shore.

Aid to the New York Central was hardly sufficient, nor was assistance to all other lines. The deficit-ridden New Haven line went bankrupt in 1961, emulating the hapless LIRR. The New York Central, despite the new cars, abandoned some of its routes and seemed prepared to drop others. Some of the equipment on these railroads dated back to World War I, and commuters were understandably unhappy with the deteriorating situation.

After officials faced the evidence of severe crisis, a government overseer was created to assume operation of all commuter services in the New York City region. Originally called the Metropolitan Commuter Transportation Authority (MCTA) in 1965, it was streamlined two years later into what is today's Metropolitan Transportation Authority (MTA). The huge agency now moves more people than any other transportation service in the country — an average of 7,000,000 *a day* on subways, buses and trains.

The first step in the shift from private to public ownership came in 1971 when the MTA purchased the New Haven Railroad lines in New York City, Westchester and Fairfield Counties.

In 1972 the MTA annexed the New York Central's Hudson and Harlem divisions with a long-term lease. Along with these routes, which extend to Poughkeepsie and Dover Plains, New York, came a lease on Grand Central Terminal in Manhattan, the last of New York City's grand depots and an architectural landmark. The Penn Central Railroad was left as the actual operator of the lines, with the MTA and Connecticut DOT administering and regulating the system. The agencies assumed financial responsibility and were compelled to swallow big deficits in addition to paying for all track upkeep. The MTA dished out $35,000,000 in subsidies for the Harlem and Hudson lines in 1976 and shared a $17.2 million deficit with the CDOT for the New Haven line.

Starting in 1976 a plan was developed which had the federal rail agency Conrail operating all the former New York Central and New Haven lines. These routes stretch like a hand across the northern suburbs. These lines were threatened again when Conrail announced that, as it considered itself primarily a freight mover, it would be phasing out passenger service. It took the intercession of Congress to insure that Conrail maintained passenger service.

But Conrail was finally ordered to divest itself of its commuter lines and in 1983 a new

135

subsidiary of the MTA — Metro-North —took over operation of the Harlem, Hudson and New Haven lines. Metro-North covers 777.8 miles of track, and is responsible for 65,000 commuters daily, 90 percent of whom pass through Grand Central Terminal.

Magnificent Grand Central Terminal, graceful symbol of an elegant era in railroad history, remains the focal point of the commuter system to the northern suburbs and Connecticut. The venerable structure sees 40,000,000 passengers a year pass under the distinctive 125-foot-high ceiling to the 421 commuter trains arriving or departing from the underground platforms. An additional 16 Amtrak passenger trains utilize Grand Central each weekday.

Leaving the terminal at 42nd Street and Lexington Avenue, all trains travel the first two miles northward in a tunnel directly under regal Park Avenue. While underground, the trains operate on 660-volt third-rail power, a vestige from the old New York Central days.

At 96th Street, the trains emerge from the tunnel portal and climb to a lofty viaduct, which carries them over the crowded neighborhoods of Spanish Harlem (El Barrio) in northern Manhattan. Many of the trains make a final city stop at the small 125th Street station before leaving Manhattan, crossing to the Bronx and thence to the suburbs.

At Mott Haven in the Bronx, just a mile beyond 125th Street, the tracks divide, sending trains off in their various directions. The Hudson line meanders along the Harlem River on the Bronx side, squeezing through a two-track cut into solid rock at Spuyten Duyvil, and then hugs the eastern bank of the broad Hudson River. The trains run on electric power to Croton-Harmon, 33 miles out of Grand Central, and then an additional 39 miles behind diesel engines to the end of the commuter route at Poughkeepsie, on the Hudson.

The second branch of the system splits off to the northeast at Mott Haven, through the Bronx to Woodlawn, 12 miles from Grand Central. There the Harlem and New Haven go their separate ways. The double-track Harlem line runs to Dover Plains, New York, 77 track-miles from the Manhattan depot.

The third primary offshoot extends 72 miles from Manhattan to New Haven. Shared for parts of its length by Amtrak's heavily-used Northeast Corridor, the New Haven line also handles traffic destined for the spurs to New Canaan, Danbury and Waterbury. The trip to New Canaan, all electrified, is eight miles out of Stamford. It is a 24-mile run from the main New Haven tracks to Waterbury, and the 27-mile branch to Waterbury makes the longest ride from Grand Central, a total of 88 miles.

The New Haven line runs through the heaviest concentrations of population and is the busiest in the Metropolitan Region. A total of 210 trains travel its routes each weekday. The Harlem Line is second with 182 trains on weekdays. The Hudson Line follows third with 130 trains. In all, the station's trains work 21 hours a day, pausing only for the early morning hours from 2 a.m. to 5 a.m. At peak hours, Grand Central hums with activity, with a train arriving or departing every minute. Some of the express and local trains carry as many as 1,200 passengers in their ten-car consist.

As for the quality of the rolling stock, the best equipment plying the Metropolitan Region rails are the two stainless steel, electrified multiple-unit types known as the M-1 Metropolitan and the M-2 Cosmopolitan-type cars. (The blue-banded M-1's actually were a design created for the LIRR, which has 770 of them.)

The 46-ton, 85-foot-long orange-banded M-2's operate in "married" pairs, like the M-1's. The M-2 differs, however, in having pantographs mounted on its roof to reach overhead wires and circuits that can accomodate the AC power of the New Haven route. The M-1's and M-2's make up three-fifths of the system's total car population.

This General Electric-manufactured stock was acquired in several shipments between 1972 and 1975. The Hudson and Harlem lines, with funding from the Port Authority, took on 178 M-1's. The New Haven received an initial shipment of 144 M-2's, and then an even 100 between 1973 and 1975. Designed efficiently, but rigidly, with fixed seats, some of which always face backwards, the cars hold 122 riders relatively comfortably.

The main line of the old New Haven Rail Road crackles with the speed of electrified MTA trains originating at Grand Central Station. — David Rubenstein

Beyond the electrified zone, the rolling stock is a contrast to the efficient newer stock. An overaged group of 17 Budd Company RDC-1's power trains on the Waterbury and Danbury branches of the New Haven line have been replaced by SPV-2000's. They also run from Brewster to Dover Plains and power the shuttles which run to Poughkeepsie. Their reliability is sporadic, it is not unusual for riders to find themselves travelling in buses while one of the engines goes in for repairs.

The longer diesel runs are powered by locomotives manufactured by Electric Motors Division. Each engine can run on either electrical or diesel power. While leaving Grand Central on the mile-long electrified tracks, it uses electrical power. Once above ground, it switches to diesel.

A MTA commuter train at Croton, N.Y. — Stan Fischler Collection

The vast yards at Croton-Harmon Station. — Stan Fischler Collection

These distinctive locomotives pull all the trains on the Hudson and New Haven routes.

Anticipating a steady growth in ridership, Metro-North has undertaken the task of expanding its fleet of 600 coaches inherited in 1983 to 731 through the 80's. In 1983 142 M-3 Budd cars were introduced on the Harlem and Hudson, where they performed poorly. Budd agreed to repair the faulty equipment at their own expense. The M-3 cars, when repaired, eliminated standees on the Hudson and Harlem lines and allowed other cars to be taken out for overhauling.

Metro-North also plans to obtain a new kind of car, called an M-4, which will complement the M-2 fleet. Instead of coming in "married pairs" like the M-1 and M-2, the M-4 car will come in threes, with the middle car interchangeable. A self-powered unit, this car will fit between two M-4 cars or a married pair of M-2's. This will make it possible to put together trains that have the exact number of cars needed for a given number of passengers.

New Bombardier-made coaches, called the Shoreliners are replacing older coaches, and the FL9 diesel locomotives will be overhauled for compatibility with the Bombardiers. However, only ten of the 33 FL9's will be in revenue service.

As for diesels, Metro-North is slowly cutting its diesel fleet, from 20 percent in 1983 to five percent by the late 1980's.

Cutting down on the diesel fleet is only one step in reducing dependence on diesel-powered equipment. The railroad is slowly extending electrification, a costly process, and over half of its 750 miles are now electrified.

In June 1984 Metro-North celebrated the completion of the $82,000,000 electrification of the Harlem line to Brewster North. The whole project included installation of welded rails (81 miles), quieter, more efficient substations, and new passenger stations built with community input on design and location.

Another program, the tie renewal program was so successful that Metro-North achieved a cycle maintenance position, with a fixed number of crossties being replaced every year, when they reach the end of their useful life.

The Park Avenue Tunnel, parts of which are nearly 150 years old, badly require rehabilitation, which it will soon obtain. Grand Central Terminal, while beautiful, suffers from chronic rush-hour congestion. To relieve this, Metro-North has plans to build two east-west passageways under 45th and 47th streets.

All of these improvement programs are being done by Metro-North under an 886-million-dollar plan called the Capital Program. Funded by federal and state monies, the Capital Program is a long-term plan to completely modernize and improve the railroad.

Despite the shortcomings, there have been visible results from the improvements. There has also been increased ridership. If nothing else, this proves both in New York and elsewhere that such a policy makes sense and pays dividends in ridership. A better system attracts passengers away from their automobiles. A few more improvements, such as adding more parking space for park-and-ride facilities, would put even more passengers on this increasingly efficient commuter transportation network.

The interior of a modern Long Island Rail Road coach, sporting a lone can of beer — definitely not factory approved!

– Stan Fischler Collection

CHAPTER 18: STUMBLING ALONG WITH THE LIRR

On a crowded Long Island Rail Road coach making its way into Manhattan not long ago, one commuter pressed by the throng against another remarked that, yes, he had in his travels encountered worse train conditions — "just outside Calcutta." The comment elicited laughs as well as a string of further unflattering comparisons from the scrunched travelers.

While often the butt of derisive jokes, what is perhaps most remarkable about the oft-maligned Long Island is that, as the busiest commuter line in the country, carrying a whopping one-fifth of all the nation's rail commuters, it is remarkably efficient. On an average weekday, the New York State-owned line will successfully transport 285,000 passengers between its 160 stations spread over 326 miles of track from Manhattan to Montauk, at the tip of Long Island, 124 miles east of the teeming metropolis.

Even with the LIRR's 714 daily trains, growing crowds strain the line's capacity. It is, in short, a railroad that despite a lifetime of notoriety is heavily used and of inestimable importance and value to the jammed Long Island suburbs. If there is an alternative to the LIRR, it is the equally packed Long Island Expressway, which, with 130,000 cars a day, or about 60 percent above its "capacity" as measured in the 1960's, presents horrors of its own and a different class of groaning sufferers. But, in a future where today's autos seem certain to become tomorrow's fossils, the LIRR can only grow in its ridership and importance. Ironically, this was thought to be the case once before, after World War II, and then the expectation proved illusory.

Following the surrender of Japan in 1945, mortgages and housing came cheap for returning GI's, and communities soon grew like weeds on Long Island. In the middle of this boom, the LIRR quickly earned the epithet as the line "everyone loves to hate." It declared bankruptcy in 1949, followed the next year by a pair of calamitous collisions.

Enraged Islanders demanded an investigation and changes. The result was the first of several studies done under government auspices. For three years, the Long Island Transit Authority analyzed the ailing railroad.

Writing in *The Passenger Train Journal*, Tom Nelligan summed up the commission's findings: "A third of the multiple unit fleet of cars was more than 35 years old, and many steam coaches were of similar vintage. Deferred maintenance was catching up." Repair and replacement, the study concluded, could be ignored no longer.

The published findings were to spur the first of several rehabilitation efforts conducted on the LIRR. The Railroad Redevelopment Corporation was set up and given $58,000,000 to spend on the LIRR over a 12-year period. It was an ambitious and necessary effort complemented by tax abatements for the Pennsylvania Railroad, which promised that it would reinvest profits from its operations into the line's improvement campaign.

Many of the older cars built before World War I were scrapped and 229 new Pullman-Standard coaches were ordered as replacements. In addition, the more heavily travelled lines were refurbished and many grade crossings — where the tracks met busy streets at the same level (grade) — were eliminated.

The last of the LIRR's steamers, a G5 type, at the Morris Park Shops in October, 1955, just two days before being taken to Nassau County's Salisbury Park for permanent museum display. — LIRR

In 1954 the LIRR came out of the bankruptcy process with a long-range guarantee of state aid to keep it on its tracks. By the mid-1960's, though, when the Railroad Redevelopment Corporation had run its course, it became obvious to then-Governor Nelson Rockefeller that the temporary boost was not enough. It was decided in 1965 that New York State would have to purchase and run the LIRR.

By an act of legislature, in 1966, the Metropolitan Commuter Transportation Authority was formed and at a cost of $65,000,000 took over the reins of the LIRR from the Pennsy. It was the first public takeover of a commuter rail line in this country, signalling a nationwide trend necessitated by problems with other commuter railroads, east and west.

Bankrolled with a hefty $2.5 billion provided through a bond issue, the MCTA, later shortened to MTA, took over the job of operating and improving the line. Two hundred billion dollars was immediately earmarked for improvements, but the total blossomed to $360,000,000 as the extent of the line's deterioration became evident. As Nelligan observed, "The MCTA took over a railroad on the verge of collapse, but at the time no one knew how bad things were about to get."

The first of several disasters came in 1968 with the arrival of the 770 new MU cars ordered from the Budd Company. In anticipation of the sleek replacements, LIRR management had neglected maintenance of its aging rolling stock, the MP54's, about to be retired. But when the new Budd cars arrived they were found unsatisfactory, performing too unreliably to undergo regular service. Budd's engineers agreed to make modifications, but meanwhile, the older cars began failing as if on cue. Without the new trains, the LIRR soon found itself with a serious equipment shortage. Operations on the busy railroad had to be cut.

On top of all that, maintenance personnel resorted to work slowdowns, which further trimmed the operating fleet. At one point, a fourth of the LIRR's cars were on blocks. Then the mechanics were joined by their brethren, the train operators, in a series of wildcat strikes. All were protesting work conditions imposed by the management in the crisis.

The Summer of 1969 was a disaster. Nelligan recalled, "At least a dozen rush-hour trains were being cancelled each day and those that ran were shorter than usual, with standee loads the rule." One journalist at the time noted that the LIRR operated "the kind of train that, if smaller, would make your little boy cry if he found it under his Christmas tree."

It took the pressure of politics in an election year for the situation to begin to untangle. Governor Rockefeller insured that differences with the unions were ironed out and emergency repairs were commenced in swift order by Budd engineers at a new Queens depot.

By the early 1970's, it seemed to a few at least that the LIRR's troubles were behind it. Nearly three-quarters of its passengers rode comfortably in new coaches travelling as fast as 80 miles per hour. At last the LIRR was running like a bona fide railroad. And then, in the Winter of 1978, it began to snow and snow — and snow.

Due to more than three feet of snow, there was a complete shutdown of the rails on February 6th and 7th. The third, or electrified, rail iced over badly, causing heavy damage to the circuits and electric motors on the MU cars. "Hundreds of passengers had to be evacuated from stalled trains," Nelligan reports of the blizzard's toll, "and when the snow stopped falling, 20 percent of the MU fleet was disabled."

As though the freak storm were a product of inept management, the public again raised an outcry about LIRR performance. The beleagured rail line had to resort to the humiliating task of distributing leaflets to irate riders, reading, "We're in bad shape and ask for your patience." Again ignmomious epithets were roundly slung at the snowed-under LIRR.

Politicians sensed the implications the disaster could have for their careers. Hearings were scheduled with an eye toward making changes at the top. Now, with Governor Hugh Carey at the helm, the investigations spurred dismissal of the LIRR's president, Robert K. Pattison, a move visible to the headhunting public. *The New York Times* speculated that the president had been dispatched to avoid his becoming a campaign liability to the powerful governor.

Yet another *gaffe* caught the LIRR in the Summer of 1978, when audits revealed the line's publicized performance data were, in fact, too good to be true. Since 1973 the railroad's on-time records had been falsified, and 1978's figure of 83 percent was calculated according to highly deceptive accounting means. Since this low point, changes on the LIRR appear to have been for the better.

In December 1981 the LIRR Five Year Capital Program was approved. This program called for improvements along the entire system. Funding would be supplied for electrification, station improvements, track and signalling improvements, as well as purchase and rehabilitation of equipment. The original program funding was $872.70 million, but this figure has since expanded considerably owing to changes in priorities and "cost refinements."

An appreciation of the size and great complexity of the LIRR system will give an idea of the job faced and how well, in relative terms, the line copes with its myriad problems. At present the LIRR laces the entire island with rails. Nine routes reach out to the suburbs from three central terminals within the boroughs of New York City.

Pennsylvania Station on Manhattan serves as the main terminal, which the LIRR shares with Amtrak and New Jersey commuter trains. More than 215 weekday trains run from Penn Station on the LIRR rails, all electric, on a 24-hour-a-day basis.

The LIRR's Brooklyn depot at Flatbush Avenue is an ancient structure. The 185 trains originating there are travelled not only by commuters working in the vicinity, but by many from Wall Street, who find it more accessible than Penn Station. An additional number join these runs at Jamaica, Queens, which also is served by the trains departing from Penn Station.

A pair of terminals are located at Hunters Point Avenue and Long Island City in Queens, north of Flatbush Avenue and east of Penn Station. These stations are utilized primarily by commuters from Manhattan, who first take the subway and then the Hunters Point connection. These stations are only used at peak hours during the week.

The eight-track Jamaica station, 11.3 miles from Penn Station, provides a major connecting point in the LIRR route system. It is the LIRR's operating center and the scene of one of the most complex train rituals of any commuter line, "the change at Jamaica."

Trains originating at each of the three terminals, heading east on different routes, pull up alongside each other at Jamaica. The middle train serves as a makeshift bridge between the other two, as passengers scuttle back and forth. LIRR regulars find the practice nothing out of the ordinary. Of course, should just one of the trains be delayed and miss the rendezvous, the consequences are obvious.

Only the Port Washington Branch, which runs east from Penn Station before elbowing up to the north shore, totally avoids the stop. This all-electric, subway-like route handles 101 trains each weekday, running to the terminus 20 miles from Manhattan.

Four other all-electric branches spike off from Jamaica on relatively short runs of up to 25 miles from Gotham. Busiest of these is the Long Beach Branch, heading to Long Island's south shore, making 72 trips on weekdays. The modern silver and blue M-1's and M-3's also make 61 trips a day to Hempstead, 31 trips to West Hempstead and 60 to Far Rockaway, west of Long Beach on Long Island's underside.

The "Main Line," so-called only because it follows the LIRR's original 19th century route to Greenport, is little-used today with the commuter zone ending generally at Yaphank, 61 miles out. Distant Greenport is serviced by but one diesel-powered train each weekday.

Diesel trains serve the remaining four LIRR routes to the relatively more isolated Long Island communities. At Mineola, one diesel branch juts northward to Oyster Bay. There are 19 regular trains each day extending to the end of this route, 35 miles eastward on the Island.

Port Jefferson, 59 miles out, is serviced by electric traction trains as far as Huntington (due to be extended to Northport), with 70 trips working to this point in the route. An additional 34 diesel runs are made eastward to the port on Long Island Sound.

The furthest Long Island station, Montauk, is connected to Gotham by an assortment of trains. On weekdays, 140 trains reach the limit of the third rail at Babylon, 38 miles from Penn Station. Diesels run 16 miles to Patchogue 18 times weekdays, with shuttles connecting further to the fashionable Hamptons, where Gatsbyesque mansions rest among the dunes.

The LIRR's rolling stock has been modernized and much of it replaced over the past decade. Although plagued with difficulties in its early days, the Budd Company's M-1 Metropolitans have since proven comfortable and reliable.

The M-1's come in permanently coupled pairs, up to 12 in a train. At 85 feet, they weigh in at 46 tons each. The design, a team effort of several engineering firms, places a 600-horsepower GE electric traction motor on an air-suspension truck.

An additional 34 electric substations had to be installed before the M-1's inaugural to allow them to run to 80 miles per hour, their regular top speed. Each is actually capable of reaching 100 miles per hour with proper track conditions. Many of the older platforms at stations have had to be rebuilt to accomodate the higher-level M-1.

The LIRR has also ordered 174 new M-3 electric passenger cars, with one car of each "married pair" equipped with "tie-down" positions for wheelchairs in addition to the refurbishing of 170 diesel-hauled coaches.

The LIRR's stock of diesel locomotives is diverse and unusual for a commuter line. It includes four types used for passenger service nowhere else. Standard EMD freight locomotives have been adapted in the form of 28 EMD GP38-2's and 23 MP15AC's.

The GP38's are usually put to use on the longer diesel runs. While doubling as freight haulers, the MP15's always find some passenger use also. This familiar train yard workhorse raises many a railroad buff's eyebrow when its bulky form is seen racing at the head of a string of commuter coaches.

The railroad also owns the last Alco cabs, whose sleek modeling make them classics. The LIRR's 19 FA-1's and FA-2's, purchased from a variety of sources in the early 1970's, are used to control trains actually powered by larger diesels in a push-pull consist. Having been modified by GE for their present use, they are not genuine locomotives in a technical sense, but still stir a thrill in the railfans as a vestige from another era of motive power.

In 1975 the LIRR acquired two Pullman-Standard and two GE-model turbine-electric cars which could function both on diesel and electricity. It was thought at the time that they would be used on lines where the third rail ended.

The trend in its coaches has, happily for the commuter, been toward all-electric, atmosphere-controlled cars. On March 9, 1979, not a soul was seen crying when the last steam-heated car was retired for good. The 118 cars working each weekday remain vulnerable, though, to many generator failures. Also, at about 25 years old for most, their age is beginning to show in an almost threadbare appearance. With 72,500,000 riders counted in 1978, and still growing, the LIRR is a large and expensive operation. An annual operating subsidy of $125 million must be provided by the MTA, a state agency. While no one denies that this is a huge figure, it breaks down to $1.75 a passenger. This compares rather favorably, for example, with the $20 subsidy per ride that the federal government must provide for Amtrak.

With more growth anticipated, a new terminus was planned within Manhattan. This fourth station is expected to be in Grand Central Terminal, on the east side, and will be served by a recently completed new tunnel under the East River at 63rd Street. Financial difficulties have delayed completion of the project, and there is no telling at this point exactly when its opening can be expected.

Another major plan is improvement of Penn Station access and equipment, including more stairways to and from platforms (as well as handicapped elevators) and a new West End concourse. These improvements would mean better passenger circulation and a relief from overcrowding.

Also in the works is a $47.9-million plan to make Penn Station into a remote-control center for Harold Interlocking, the network of tracks, switches and signals in Long Island City. Harold is responsible for routing all train movements to and from Penn Station and Hunterspoint Avenue, as well as Amtrak's Northeast Corridor service. It is an antiquated system and requires redesigning, installation of the necessary improvements and provisions for the remoting to Penn Station.

The switching systems and towers in Penn Station, which date from 1910, will be modernized and remotely controlled from a new control room. These plans will be undertaken with Amtrak, under a Joint Venture Agreement.

Nearing completion is the reconstruction of the West Side Yard, which will store up to 320 M-1 and M-3 cars and provide facilities for inspections and light repairs. Morning trains going to Penn Station would continue west to the yard, while evening trains would come from the yard to Penn Station and continue east. This would mean less tunnel congestion because one East River Tunnel would be freed from carrying the non-revenue trains from Penn Station. The yard, coupled with the improvements at Penn, would mean an increase in track capacity by a minimum of 25 percent.

The Main Line track between Jamaica and Penn Station is going to receive automatic speed control and reverse signalling. So far, one block of reverse signalling has been completed on the Main Line No. 2 eastbound track.

The Port Jefferson branch, the most heavily travelled line on the LIRR, is slated to receive a second electrified main track between Ammot Interlocking (east of Syosset) and Huntington, and extension of electrification along the existing track between Huntington and Northport. Improvements in track, signals, substations and stations will also be performed along with electrification.

The fast-growing Ronkonkoma line will have electrification extended from Hicksville to Ronkonkoma, along with installation of an aerial signal power line. Ronkonkoma Yard will also be relocated. These improvements will service 6,700 who ride the westbound line daily during the a.m. peak period, a ridership increase of 60 percent since 1972.

Under the Capital Program rails, ties and ballast approximately 60 years old (far in excess of the 50-year service life of rail, and the 35 years for tie) will be replaced, and the third rail that has been in service since 1910 (and should be replaced every 50 years) will also be replaced.

The LIRR has entered a new era. A new president, Bruce C. McIver, was appointed by the MTA to replace the incumbent Robin Wilson. McIver, formerly a labor negotiator for the city and the MTA, is credited with helping to bring about several positive changes at the LIRR, something people hope he can continue.

New cars, new stations and new planning — it will probably take all this and more to stem the tide of invective heard at the platform when the inevitable announcement of yet another delayed train comes over the loudspeaker. Many are impatient, although many have a better-late-than-never attitude. Complain as they might, stumbling along with the LIRR, these faithful riders are joined every day by more on this unique commuter railroad, which will be a necessity for, it seems, a great while longer.

Few commuter cars performed more reliably or for a longer time than the Lackawanna electrics shown here. — Stan Fischler Collection

CHAPTER 19: THE JERSEY BOUNCE

The gag in the mid-1960's went like this: there are three deterrents to a population explosion; war, pestilence and the New Jersey Turnpike!

Residents of the nation's most densely populated state treat their foremost ribbon of concrete with black humor — and for good reason. The Turnpike, along with the Garden State Parkway, George Washington Bridge and Lincoln and Holland tunnels, has emerged as a thouroughfare producing as much trouble as value. Not the efficient people-movers originally envisioned, these routes doomed the state's commuter railroads, once an effective means of mass transportation.

One by one commuter mainstays disappeared from the New Jersey landscape. In 1957 the Erie closed its Jersey City terminal and moved in with the Delaware, Lackawanna and Western at Hoboken. The Pennsylvania Railroad shuttered its Exchange Place (Jersey City) depot in 1961. The tiny New York, Susquehanna and Western Railroad, which carried passengers to such towns as Sussex, Hanford, Stillwater, Blairstown and Hainesburg, New Jersey, went out of the passenger business in 1966. The New York Central's West Shore Line, which ran north through New Jersey, also threw in the towel.

The survivors weren't in very good shape either. By the start of the 1960's the Lackawanna's suburban line was losing $2,000,000 a year and the line was desperately trying to get out of the commuter railroad business. In this case, at least, there were sweet uses for the adversity. The line's bid to discontinue passenger service caused a ripple all the way to the state capitol in Trenton, where Governor Robert B. Meyner agreed to forge a pro-mass transit platform. The first tangible evidence of support was a $1,300,000 grant to the Central Railroad of New Jersey, followed by another subsidy for the Lackawanna and the Pennsy. Meyner made certain that a clause was inserted providing that the contracts would be renewed annually through 1970.

Although the subsidies provided a flicker of hope, they hardly offered enough financial aid to afford fiscal comfort. The Erie and Lackawanna, whose marriage produced the Erie-Lackawanna, hardly prospered in their unity. The deficit in 1966 on passenger operations totalled a whopping $12,000,000, mostly because of the suburban trains, but also included the Hudson River ferries. The Erie-Lackawanna informed the state that its commuter lines had had it. A bid was made in Trenton to have all suburban lines eliminated. Unfortunately for commuters, the EL did get half of what it suggested — of the 298 trains, 143 were eliminated.

But in 1965 Governor Richard Hughes was up for re-election. After viewing the disarray into which the commuter lines had fallen, Hughes campaigned in favor of greater state involvement in suburban rail transit. He argued that government operation of the commuter lines was "an inescapable final solution." Hughes' opponent in the election took an opposing stance, insisting that instead of the state funding the money-losing lines, the private operators either make it — or go broke — on their own.

Hughes triumphed and then made good on his promise. His major effort was a ten-year program for sustaining the commuter lines. The tab of $375,000,000 covered such necessities as new rolling stock which, wonder of wonders, would be air-conditioned. With the elimination of

The Susquehanna's self-contained commuter car heads for Jersey City.

– Stan Fischler Collection

Central Railroad of New Jersey ferry terminal. — courtesy John Krause

the Hudson River ferries, it was agreed that arrangements should be made for direct connections for the Jersey Central and Erie-Lackawanna to Manhattan.

Proving he meant business, Hughes made provisions for a State Department of Transportation, which would orchestrate his program through a Commuter Operating Agency. At last the beleagured riders could look ahead with a trace of optimism. After weathering a court challenge, the Hughes' program was set in motion early in 1967, thereby erasing fears that the existing three commuter railroads in northern New Jersey would be wiped out. But that was only a step in the right direction. The great leap forward was yet to come.

What many experts believed was needed to adequately merge the various rail services was an elaborate blueprint which included the elimination of peripheral operations while speeding up existing practical services. The result was the "Aldene Plan," a $3,600,000 project which meshed many of the necessary components of the surviving commuter lines while erasing others deemed nonessential, although the term is a relative one depending on perspective.

The day the "Aldene Plan" went into effect, April 30, 1967, the Jersey Central shuttered its ferry terminal and Jersey City rail depot. The CNJ trains henceforth would operate out of Pennsylvania Station in Newark, forging a link between the Jersey Central and the Hudson Tubes. A year later the Erie-Lackawanna trans-Hudson ferries were discontinued.

Built in 1907, the Lackawanna Rail Road Ferry Terminal at Hoboken linked directly with the adjacent train terminal. — Stan Fischler Collection

One feature of the "Aldene Plan" was replacement of decrepit rolling stock. New diesels were purchased, as well as a fleet of new, streamlined passenger cars for the Hudson Tubes. Those venerable coaches deemed worthy of maintaining into the 1970's were set aside for renovation and utilized in a push-pull service.

New funds also were forthcoming, enough to offset the bankruptcy petition filed by the Jersey Central. New Jersey came through with $2,000,000 to keep the CNJ operable. The Erie-Lackawanna was not ignored either, and infused with funds for restoration of 45 of the 143 trains previously eliminated in the 1966 cutbacks.

To facilitate movement of passengers, the Hudson Tubes (taken over by the interstate governmental agency, the New York-New Jersey Port Authority and now known as PATH) established a one-fare system throughout the line, whereas in the past the trip to Newark required an additional fare. Suitable alterations were made to handle the one-fare policy. Turnstiles were installed and fences built at the New York-bound track at Pennsylvania Station in Newark.

Other advantages of the Port Authority of New York and New Jersey takeover were immediately evident. The Tubes trains gained exclusive track rights — isolating them from Pennsylvania tracks — and utilized the third rail. The rolling stock, which once employed a cab signal system similar to the Pennsylvania Railroad, no longer was obligatory on the PATH Tubes. More and more, the Tubes took on the trappings of the mass transit king of North America, the New York City subway. A feature which New York straphangers took for granted, the safety tripping device which prevented rear-end crashes, soon became *de rigueur* on the Tubes. Another innovation, borrowed from the New York system, was the implementation of distinctive color symbols for

The PATH Journal Square station within the Transportation Center is the midpoint for trips between Newark and lower and midtown Manhattan. The completely rebuilt facilities now serve more than 32,000 passengers a day.   – Port Authority of NY and NJ

each of the Tubes' assorted routes. Not surprisingly, ridership on the Tubes climbed following implementation of the "Aldene Plan" and the ensuing improvements. Yet the financial problems remained.

Compare the turn-of-the-century artist's view of what the Tube's Jersey City connection would be like with the real thing 85 years later. Note the twin towers of the World Trade Center in Manhattan, where the trains begin their run to New Jersey.

– Stan Fischler Collection

The modern equipment featured air conditioning, huge windows and a variety of seating.
– Port Authority of NY and NJ

The northernmost terminus of the Tubes is 33rd Street (Herald Square), where Macy's faces Gimbels.
– Stan Fischler Collection

The train slows down at the yard south of Newark. — Stan Fischler Collection

The World Trade Center terminal is one of the busiest commuter stations in the world.
— Stan Fischler Collection

PATH rolling stock is among the best-maintained of any commuter railroad on the continent.
– Stan Fischler Collection

The Tubes have employed sophisticated technology in their control center at Journal Square, Jersey City. The installation was opened in 1980. — Stan Fischler Collection

Like virtually all transit systems in North America, the Tubes was unable to meet the operating deficit from its turnstile revenue. "The full extent of the fiscal and social dilemma this represents," wrote Brian Cudahy in *Rails Under The Mighty Hudson*, "can be seen in the fact that, while total ridership on the system is about a third of its all-time high, ridership during the peak rush-hour periods is now heavier than it ever was in H&M history . . . The PATH system is in the curious position of not carrying enough passengers to break even, but also not having enough capacity to handle rush-hour crowds."

Making do with its available trackage, the Port Authority appears to be making an honest effort to keep the Tubes in reasonable shape. New rolling stock was ordered and installed in the early 1970's, giving the line a spiffy look to go with its commendable performance. Coupled with its 75-cent fare, the PATH provides one of the best buys in commuter transit on the continent.

The Tubes was not the only beneficiary of modern equipment. Prior to the Pennsylvania's merger with the New York Central to form Penn Central, the Pennsy ordered 35 high-speed, 85-foot multiple-unit cars from the St. Louis Car Company at a cost of $10,000,000. The new cars were dubbed Jersey Arrows and placed on the New York-Trenton run when delivered in 1968.

With groundwork laid for a rejuvenated commuter system, public opinion began to gradually sway in the direction of permanent subsidization of the metropolitan area railroads. In 1968 New Jersey voters were put to the test on the issue and responded on the side of the trains.

The New Jersey electorate okayed a $200,000,000 transit bond issue providing for additional improvements. The feds in Washington then provided matching funds and still more equipment arrived on the scene, although it was quite evident that some lines would get more attention than others.

According to experts on the commuter scene, such as author Tom Nelligan, the Erie-Lackawanna and Penn Central suburban lines received the most attention. "Between 1971 and 1973," commented Nelligan, "Erie-Lackawanna diesel service was completely re-equipped with 155 Pullman-Standard push-pull cars. The state bought 70 high-speed multiple units for the Penn Central. Known as Jersey Arrow II's, they were delivered by General Electric in 1974 and 1975."

Through it all, the Jersey Central remained the step-child in terms of improved rolling stock. Instead of obtaining fresh-off-the-assembly-line cars, the CNJ was presented with previously-owned coaches which formerly rolled on the tracks of the Burlington Northern and Santa Fe lines. "The Burlington Northern cars," wrote Nelligan in *Passenger Train Journal*, "retained their original paint for several years. They were Burlington Northern consists that looked like hopelessly lost 'Empire Builders'."

The CNJ's roadbed fared better than the trains themselves. In 1974 the Jersey Central received a $2,700,000 appropriation for overhauling the main line's trackwork. For the moment, at least, all seemed rosy in the immediate future for the commuter lines. Then, along came Conrail and all hell broke loose.

When Washington, D.C., mandated a federally-supported railroad (Conrail), the New Jersey lines — like it or not — were swallowed up by the artificially-contrived goliath. Thus, on April 1, 1976, when Conrail went in business for itself, the Jersey Central, Erie-Lackawanna and Penn Central suddenly found themselves wearing the Conrail decal. Much to the dismay of commuters savoring the renaissance of their suburban lines, riders soon learned that Conrail cared as much about upgrading passenger lines as did implacable foes such as Greyhound Bus Lines. Late in 1976 suspicions of the cynics were confirmed when it was learned that Conrail planned, in 1977, to cancel the operating contracts which had been signed with its predecessor companies.

This meant war as far as the commuters and the State Department of Transportation were concerned. To thwart Conrail, the state went to court and won a federal court injunction forbidding Conrail from unilaterally terminating the trains. Meanwhile, Congress responded to grassroots reaction and sought to hammer out a plan which would save the commuter lines. With New Jersey Senator Harrison Williams leading the charge, Congress passed a Williams-sponsored

Wide, contoured seats on the N.J. Arrow II cars help assure a comfortable ride for commuters.
– photo courtesy G.E.

New Jersey Arrow II commuter cars are made of stainless steel and can travel up to 100 miles an hour. They were produced for NJ DOT by the General Electric Company, Erie, Pa.
–photo courtesy G.E.

bill requiring Conrail to operate commuter service for any local line that could pay for it. Conrail was defeated and Jersey's suburban lines were saved. There were more equipment purchases: in 1976 an $187,700,000 outlay went for 230 high-speed Jersey Arrow III cars. In December 1976, in one of the most formidable transactions, the New Jersey Department of Transportation purchased rolling stock from Conrail.

This was followed with an even more significant purchase in 1978, when for only $17,000,000 the state transportation department annexed the lines themselves. Now New Jersey, like Connecticut and New York, owned the tracks and equipment of its commuter lines. (The one exception was Amtrak's New York-to-Trenton run, a 58-mile segment once part of the Penn Central and now on the main line of the Northeast Corridor rail operation.)

To the commuter these developments were a marvel, but to the transportation critic they seemed too little, too late. Lawrence Grow was one of those skeptics. In his book *On the 8:02*, he commented, "Everyone realizes now that the subsidy program should have started much earlier. Instead, the state put all of its transportation dollars into highways and pollution. In this respect, New Jersey was by no means exceptional, but in the most densely populated state in the nation the effect was particularly toxic."

Finally, in 1979, on order from Congress, Conrail divested itself of its commuter lines and the state took complete control. A new agency, New Jersey Transit, was created and took over rail and bus service in 1983. In an effort to correct the deplorable state that the commuter lines had fallen into, the new agency started a capital program amounting to $1,133.2 million. The money has helped New Jersey lines to move from the dilapidation of the 70's to a far more efficient operation in the 80's. The improvements even prompted the American Public Transit Association to give N.J. Transit an Outstanding Achievement Award in 1984.

The old and the new at Hoboken Terminal. — Stan Fischler Collection

While the 1970's proved considerably less than a banner decade for CNJ riders, the state transportation department offered hope for the future, including the other lines in the state, especially the former Delaware, Lackawanna and Western emanating from Hoboken. The most frequently used of these lines is the Morris and Essex Line from Hoboken to Dover, New Jersey, complemented by branches to Montclair and Gladstone. As noted earlier, these routes were electrified in 1930 and 1931, and the DL&W then bought a fleet of 141 passenger coaches from the Pullman Company. *These same cars remained in service through 1980!* This line has finally received modern equipment and re-electrification of the M&E has been done at a cost of $449 million.

In addition to the electrics, the Hoboken terminal dispatches a number of diesels to an assortment of destinations. One of them is the Pascack Valley Line to Spring Valley, New York, and there is the former Erie Main Line to Suffern and Port Jervis, New York, as well as the former DL&W Boonton Line to Dover and Netcong, New Jersey.

According to transit critic Tom Nelligan, the New Jersey transportation department's masterpiece is the run along Amtrak's Northeast Corridor, formerly the Pennsylvania Railroad's main line between New York and Philadelphia. The State Transportation Department operates 76 main line multiple-unit-type trains along the Corridor, as well as the 42 Amtrak trains which take on local passengers. Of these trains, the state operates 21 trains each way between Penn Station and New Brunswick, as well as 17 trains to the state capital, Trenton. Rolling stock consists of the relatively new and speedy Jersey Arrow, multiple-unit electric cars which have been known to exceed speeds of 80 miles per hour. The good, high-speed equipment has resulted in an increase in ridership.

Running off from the Corridor is a Toonerville-like shuttle to Princeton serviced by one Jersey Arrow. It rolls for only three miles, linking the university and town with Princeton Junction for 20 trips a day.

Among the least-heralded of the state-operated commuter lines in New Jersey is the North Jersey Coast Line, originally the New York and Long Branch. In its heyday, the New York and Long Branch was co-operated by the Pennsy and Jersey Central and offered great potential for future commuter development. But the lines cut service at a critical time following World War II, just as the communities began to balloon with new residents.

Fortunately, the State of New Jersey saved the line from extinction and today electrified coaches ply a route between Pennsylvania Station and Matawan, where the electrification ends. Diesels emanating from both Newark and New York roll beyond Matawan to the southern terminus at Bay Head.

The North Jersey Coast Line has only recently begun receiving attention. Formerly the bane of New Jersey commuters, the line was finally electrified from South Amboy to Matawan, and there are plans for further electrification. Rolling stock — which included discards from such diverse carriers as the Missouri Pacific; Kansas City Southern; Burlington Northern; Atchison, Topeka and Santa Fe; as well as some converted Pullmans from the Pennsylvania — was replaced with modern equipment.

Under the capital program New Jersey Transit plans to renovate 60 stations, as well as the Hoboken Terminal, Newark Penn Station and Broad Street Station in Newark. They have also placed 17 new diesel locomotives and 117 new rail cars into service. NJ Transit has altogether some 176 plans to put into action.

An enterprising blueprint calls for an arrangement whereby former Erie-Lackawanna, rather than terminating at Hoboken, would use Manhattan's Pennsylvania Station as their depot. This would be made possible by means of a coupling of the EL and former Pennsy lines at a location near Kearny, New Jersey. A trifle less far-fetched is a plan for linking the erstwhile Erie and Lackawanna trains at Montclair, New Jersey. For this to be converted from the drawing board to reality will require electrification of the onetime Erie tracks. Unless that happens, the trains plying the old Erie routes will continue to use the venerable Hoboken depot.

With a little bit of luck and a lot of dollars, embattled commuters on the North Jersey Coast Line will eventually get their wish for further electrification of the line up to Red Bank. Renovation of stations along the way is part of the plan to upgrade that presently unappealing run.

Author and transit critic Tom Nelligan is one who believes that the state has no choice but to endorse the modernization plans for the suburban lines. "It is impossible," said Nelligan, "to imagine how the state could accomodate any shrinkage of the basic New Jersey Department of Transportation system. The state's highways are among the most crowded in the country. They are incapable of absorbing any additional rush-hour traffic and the air is incapable of dispersing any additional automotive pollution. Politically, it is unlikely that either the governor or the legislature could seriously advocate scrapping NJDOT. The problem is that at least two areas of the system seem to be spontaneously scrapping themselves."

There is, however, hope, thanks to the inevitable decline and fall of the private automobile. "There are bright spots," Nelligan concluded in a report to *The Passenger Train Journal*. "Patronage on the ex-Penn Central trains into Penn Station is increasing at about eight per cent a year, and the Hoboken diesel lines are holding up.

"New Jersey's commuter railroads survived the decline of the 1950's to begin a comeback in the 1970's. With a bit of luck, and support from the voters, that comeback can continue."

Ridership is up on the New Jersey Transit rail lines, thanks to new rolling stock like these high performance cars. — Stan Fischler Collection

A GUIDE TO KNOWING AND ENJOYING THE TRI-STATE COMMUTER RAIL LINES

New York City's commuter rail web has, over the past century and a half, grown to include 32 lines, snaking out of such diverse terminals as Grand Central, Penn Station, Gimbel's Basement in Manhattan, Flatbush Avenue in Brooklyn, and Hoboken's venerable New Jersey Transit rail hub across the Hudson from Manhattan. More than 621,000 riders use the commuter lines daily; some under the flag of the Metropolitan Transportation Authority, others under the NJ Transit banner. Few but the most stoic, or the rail buffs, enjoy the experience. Nevertheless, New York boasts one of the most comprehensive commuter networks in the world. The state-operated MTA operates 791 route miles, embracing the Long Island, Metro-North and Staten Island Rapid Transit, as well as the New York subways. Metro-North, a new MTA operating subsidy, operates trains on the Harlem, Hudson and New Haven lines. The New Haven line is operated under contract with the Connecticut Department of Transportation.

N.J. Transit orchestrates New Jersey's commuter trains on 420 miles of track. These include routes formerly owned by the Erie-Lackawanna, Central Railroad of New Jersey, Reading, New York and Long Branch, and Penn Central. Finally, the Port of New York Authority runs 1,100 trains a day on its PATH (formerly the Hudson and Manhattan) tracks under the Hudson and on to such points as Newark, Hoboken and Jersey City.

The commuter rail labyrinth offers 811 rush-hour trains, reaching speeds as high as 80 miles per hour. Unlike its MTA cousin, the New York subways, the commuter lines are virtually graffitti-free and feature a low crime rate. They also are a bargain, especially the PATH Tubes, with its distinctive 19th century wine cellar aroma and 75-cent ride that'll get you all the way from 33rd Street, Manhattan, to Newark at a fraction of the cost for an equivalent taxi ride.

For the daily commuter, the Metropolitan Area's rail system is hated for its old equipment, rough ride, lateness, and rush-hour crowding. But for the train buff, there is an endless source of goodies in the commuter rail cornucopia. To the train lover, the ride is the thing, and here, from the railfan's viewpoint, is how we rate the lines:

* **** Highest rating
* *** Among the best
* ** Good, but not that good
* * Even a railfan would pass it by

NEW JERSEY TRANSIT

*** ***Main-Bergen County Line***. Hoboken to Suffern, New York. Running time, 57 minutes. Slicing across booming Bergen County, this EL standby concludes its run at Glen Rock, where it meets the main line to Port Jervis, New York. Short but sweet — and featuring modern equipment — the Bergen County portion clicks through wooded Radburn, wide-streeted Ridgewood and sleepy Glen Rock. There are two Glen Rock stations. One is a holdover from the old Erie days when the main line ran all the way to Chicago.

   *** **Main Line**. Hoboken, New Jersey, to Port Jervis, New York. Running time, two hours and 21 minutes. Thoreau would have enjoyed the transition from a blue-collar suburban ride to the pastoral surroundings north of Tuxedo, New York. The homestretch links Goshen's horse farms and Port Jervis' unique tri-state (Pennsylvania, New Jersey, New York) setting. A minus is the spate of junkyards and dumps near Clifton, Passaic and Delawanna.

   ** **Pascack Valley Line**. Hoboken, New Jersey to Spring Valley, New York. Running time, one hour, eight minutes. Once Spring Valley was a mini-Borscht Belt, now it's another slice of suburbia served by NJ Transit's push-pull trains. The northerly run from Westwood to the finish is pleasant enough, but this is not a recommended excursion because of the inability to complete the round-trip, starting from Hoboken in the morning.

   ** **Boonton Line**. Hoboken to Netcong, New Jersey. Running time, one hour, 23 minutes. This is the line built for royalty. Equipment is in mint condition (push-pull) and so is the scenery, especially the mountain lakes sector. Apart from a rather bumpy rumble at the entrance to Wayne, the ride is smooth and often interesting. A must stop is Glen Ridge, to visit the Erie-Lackawanna Railroad Museum adjacent to the station. Boonton also sports a neat curio at the sides of the tracks; 13 colorfully redecorated Long Island Rail Road cars from a bygone era, now posing as boutiques and assorted other cutsie shops. The aspect that deprives the Boonton Line from a four-star rating is scheduling. *It is impossible to make a round-trip expedition to the end of the line in one day* if you leave from Hoboken. (Instead, get off before the end of the line at Dover and change to the electric M-U train for the ride back). Handsome stations are sprinkled throughout the system, complementing the area's posh homes.

   * **Montclair Branch, Morris and Essex Lines**. Hoboken to Montclair, New Jersey. Running time 28 minutes. If ever a case could be made for the automobile, this product of the old Delaware, Lackawanna and Western makes it. Shuttered factories, garbage and graffitti-covered stations line the route across Northern New Jersey. If you're lucky, you might encounter a pleasant engineer to chat with, otherwise arm yourself with a book, magazine or newspaper — preferably with large print.

*** ***Morristown Line, Morris and Essex Line***. Hoboken to Dover, New Jersey. Running time, one hour, six minutes. Built in 1907 as a combined ferry-railroad terminal, the Hoboken junction has retained much of its early flavor. Although the ferry to Manhattan was abandoned in 1967, the classic tidewater terminal remains with its ferry slips, two-level concourse and rotted timbers. The high-roofed cars dating back to 1915 were replaced in 1984 by Arrow cars. Just past Short Hills, the first superb view of Manhattan is available. En route to Morristown, the train rambles past a number of lakes and ponds frequented by fisherman.

** ***Gladstone Branch, Morris and Essex Lines***. Hoboken to Gladstone, New Jersey. Running time, one hour, 17 minutes. Regular commuters should appreciate the single track line with its new structures as well as the new coaches. The scenic route is graced by five crossings of the Passaic River — one with a long trestle — the Hondailee Quarry and flocks of swans between Bernardsville and Far Hills.

*** ***North East Corridor Line***. Pennsylvania Station to Trenton, New Jersey. Running time, one hour, 20 minutes. The benefits of federal funding are apparent, especially south of Newark, where the welded rails are so smooth you can hand-write a letter without trauma. Streamlined stainless steel center-entrance doors complement the high- and low-level vestibule doors, all of which permit quick boarding. The St. Louis-built equipment not only has a readable map, but a public address system and high-back contoured seats. The Trenton terminal, although a new building, could be better maintained. A more impressive station vista is the antediluvian Elizabeth Jersey Central terminal, where the clocks in the tower have frozen time at 7:10. Finally, for a real train lover's treat, stand at the front window and watch a Metroliner approach from the opposite direction.

** ***North Jersey Coast Line***. Pennsylvania Station to Matawan, New Jersey. Running time, 56 minutes. Once the Penn Central line, this New Jersey Transit offering is fast, clean and effective, although not especially recommended for the casual railfan. Nothing about the brief spin to Matawan is entertaining or distinctive, apart from the impressive bridge over the Raritan River. Train buffs who go this route should continue from the Matawan electric train on to the diesel bound for Bay Head.

**** ***Bay Head Branch, North Jersey Coast Line***. Newark to Bay Head Junction, New Jersey. Running time, two hours, two minutes. For a taste of New England in Jersey take this former New York and Long Branch line with a unique flavor that will titillate railfans. Rolling out of Newark, the trains are among the more colorful in the area, among them displaced Burlington Northern Railroad intercity coaches (many with their original GN colors), including the once-venerated *Empire Builder*. Coaches are clean, the ride is smooth and quiet, and the dull roar of the diesel seems to complement the occasional blare of an air horn. The best part of the expedition begins after crossing the Raritan River. The train skirts the Atlantic coast line (at one point the tracks are on the beach), passing salt marshes, stands of scrub oak and a sprinkling of salt water inlets, the best of which is at Matawan. Adding to the effect are restored stations at Red Bank (gingerbread) and Spring Lake, and middle-American hamlets such as Little Silver, Elberon and Long Branch. The vista at Point Pleasant Beach can match anything New England has to offer. Restaurants are plentiful at the railhead.

*** ***Raritan Valley Line***. Newark, New Jersey to High Bridge. Running time, two hours, ten minutes. This is blue plate special commuting. One of the best 34-minute gallops is achieved between Newark and Bound Brook over a well-manicured roadbed. Heading west past the Raritan River, the eye is soothed by lush farmland, followed by rolling hills.

LONG ISLAND RAIL ROAD

** *Atlantic Branch*. Flatbush Avenue, Brooklyn, to Jamaica, Queens. Running time, 19 minutes. Railfans will love this sleeper. It emerges from the venerable downtown (opened 1905) Brooklyn terminal to burst into open air at Bedford Avenue, climbing to a steel elevated trestle at Nostrand Avenue. From this point, until it re-enters the portal at the Bedford-Stuyvesant border, the Atlantic branch offers rare sounds and sights. The special sound is generated by the unusually high speed (remember, this is a *railroad*, not a mere subway) on the elevated track. Adding to the thrill is the fact that no guardrail or walkways are located on the far (right) side of the tracks. As a result, passengers sitting on the outside right window seats get the impression by looking out the window that there is nothing but a train floating on air, since nothing can be seen below but the street. Having re-entered the tunnel, the train whooshes to Jamaica under Atlantic Avenue at 80 mph. Until around 1940 the trains ran at street level *along* Atlantic Avenue. On the debit side is the depressing vista of ravaged Bed-Stuy on both sides of the elevated tracks. Gourmets will consider it imperative to stop at Brooklyn's best seafood restaurant, Gage & Tollner's on Fulton Street, about 15 minutes walk from Flatbush Avenue Terminal.

** *West Hempstead Branch*. Valley Stream to West Hempstead, New York. Running time, 16 minutes. A classic bedroom suburb spur, this run bounces langorously through Westwood, Malverne, Lakeview, Hempstead Gardens and West Hempstead. Heavily-wooded Westwood and Malverne, boasting a village green, are the most arboreous of the stops.

* *Hempstead Branch*. Floral Park to Hempstead, New York. Running time, 16 minutes. For those who enjoy inspecting other people's backyards, the Hempstead line faces a lot of clothes lines. It also features an unspectacular but amiable run through Stewart Manor and self-important Garden City, within sight of Adelphi University, and an unusual station named Country Life Press. The big downer occurs at the last stop, Hempstead, a block from the ultra-seedy Hempstead bus depot.

* *Far Rockaway Branch*. Pennsylvania Station to Far Rockaway, New York. Running time, 52 minutes (some rush-hour expresses have made it in 46 minutes). The line is strong on backyards and weak on other scenic values. Admirers of 90-degree curves will be pleased with one majestic view of the Manhattan skyline. Otherwise, ignore it unless you live in Far Rockaway.

* *Long Beach Branch*. Pennsylvania Station to Long Beach, New York. Running time, 50 minutes. The rickety Reynolds Channel trestle provides the brief sensation of a thrill ride. So far, the span has yet to collapse, but will be rebuilt by 1988. Otherwise the Long Beach line, eventually to be rehabilitated, is as dull as tract housing. On the plus side is the nifty sand beach, but that's reserved (unless you're crafty) for local residents.

*** *Port Washington*. Pennsylvania Station to Port Washington, New York. Running time, 45 minutes. Dashing Dan never had it so good. Missing the irksome "change at Jamaica," the Port Washington run sports spanking new and clean equipment to serve the heavily-wooded North Shore of Long Island. Port Washington is an especially pleasant town for walking, with the possibility of a jaunt to Manhasset Bay or the shopping center.

*** *Oyster Bay Branch*. Pennsylvania Station to Oyster Bay, New York. Running time, one hour and 17 minutes. Battleship gray, old multiple-unit (MU) rolling stock provides stark contrast to the travelogue settings of stops such as Sea Cliff and Oyster Bay. Sea Cliff is dotted with preserved Victorian homes, while Oyster Bay is the site of Sagamore Hill, home of President Teddy Roosevelt. An LIRR conductor confided that the Oyster Bay Line once was burdened with inferior equipment in retribution for complaints lodged by an Oyster Bay commuter. The LIRR is conducting an interesting study to test the feasibility of converting this branch to light rail.

* *Babylon Branch*. Penn Station to Babylon. Running time, one hour. Serving the largest commuter populace of any line in the country, and providing the highest frequency of service on the Long Island Rail Road, the Babylon line rates as a "utility" line, but little more. For ten stops in Nassau County, the Babylon line parallels Sunrise Highway, one of Long Island's busiest and ugliest thoroughfares. Shifting southward in Suffolk County, the branch stops at Amityville, Copiague and Lindenhurst before coming to rest at Babylon, near Montauk Highway, Long Island's southernmost route.

** **Port Jefferson Branch**. Pennsylvania Station to Port Jefferson, New York. Running time, two hours, 4 minutes. One of the LIRR's most schizophrenic routes, Port Jefferson vacillates from beautiful (St. James' woods and farms) to beastly (Hicksville's warehouses and factories) while remaining consistently taxing to the body. Heading east, riders switch from modern electric trains to diesel-hauled antiques at Huntington. On the plus side is charming Port Jefferson, the Woodstock of Suffolk County, with its sprinkling (on Route 25A) of restaurants, boutiques, craft and antique shops.

** **Montauk Branch**. Pennsylvania Station to Montauk, New York. Running time, three hours, 49 minutes. Imagine yourself riding to Albany on continuous welded rail in rebuilt cars and you have an idea of this 120-mile meander through Nassau to the eastern tip of Suffolk County. It's a glorious ride through duck farms and on to the dunes of the Hamptons. A glorious view of the sun over the Hamptons is almost worth the trip.

* **Ronkonkoma Branch**. Pennsylvania Station to Ronkonkoma, New York. Running time, one hour, 35 minutes. The first line to snake its way into Suffolk County (1843), the Ronkonkoma Branch has little else to commend it unless your tastes run to industrial parks, weed-covered fields and row houses. Electrification is in the works.

** **Greenport Branch**. Pennsylvania Station to Greenport, New York. Running time, three hours, six minutes. A typical LIRR point-counterpoint. On the minus side were filthy cars, which have since been refurbished, and the right-of-way that remains so rough that reading is virtually impossible. But the Greenport division has its plusses, not the least of which is a heritage. In 1844, near Manorville, an Irish immigrant track gang drove the last spike to complete what had been envisioned as a New York-Boston rail-ship link. The plan was scuttled in 1850 when, instead, the Boston-New York coupling was made by rail via Connecticut. As a result, Greenport remains a modest town rather than a metropolis. The railhead is just a few feet from Gardiner's Bay and the ferry to Shelter Island. If you don't mind the messy rolling stock (toilet included), there are enough quaint towns to make the path to Greenport worthwhile.

METRO-NORTH

*** **New Haven Line**. Grand Central Station to New Haven, Connecticut. Running time, one hour, 35 minutes. Dashing under Park Avenue, the train emerges at 96th Street and passes the rejuvenating Harlem and "El Barrio" (Spanish Harlem) before crossing the East River for a jaunt through the Bronx. The ride accelerates in every way until it reaches its visual peak kissing the Connecticut coast line. As commuter runs go, this one is most like a big-time operation. (Special Note for Railfans: the world-famous Shoreline Trolley Museum is located in the suburbs of New Haven and should not be missed. Trolleys run daily during the summer.)

*** **New Canaan Branch**. Grand Central Station to New Canaan, Connecticut. Running time, one hour, four minutes. From Grand Central to Stamford, the Cosmopolitan (M-2) cars operate over newly-installed, continuously welded rail. While this eliminates the traditional (and beloved) clickety-clack of wheel over rail-gaps, it provides an unusually smooth ride and high speeds, even around curves, as high as 70 mph in some areas. Rail advocates delight in watching the Cosmopolitans overtake auto traffic on the adjacent I-95 superhighway. The high-speed run ends at Stamford, where a change is made to the eight-mile shuttle that makes like a trolley car as it bisects woodlands and expansive suburbia en route to New Canaan. As the train horn sounds at the many unguarded crossings, one gets the impression that cartoonist Fontaine Fox used this branch as his prototype for "the Toonerville folks" comic strip of bygone years. New Canaan, itself, makes the trip worthwhile. An animated Currier and Ives town, New Canaan boasts a magnificent station and appealing shops along Elm and Main streets.

** ***Waterbury Branch***. Grand Central Station to Waterbury, Connecticut. Running time, two hours, ten minutes. Another Jekyll-Hyde of the rails, the Waterbury Branch starts out like gangbusters, with sleek, speedy Cosmopolitan (M-2) cars plying the New Haven Line to Bridgeport. Skimming alongside the southern Connecticut coastline, the electric-powered cars are greeted by egrets, swans and the ubiquitous gulls until it's time to change at Bridgeport. Then it's on to Connecticut's answer to the old interurban trolleys. The rolling stock consists of one RDC, put on the line in 1983, which parallels the Naugutuck River en route to Shelton, Derby, Ansonia, Seymour and Naugatuck. Tracks in this portion of the route are horribly bumpy and only the river views provide an antidote to the discomfort.

*** ***Danbury Branch***. Grand Central Terminal to Danbury, Connecticut. Running time, one hour, 54 minutes. A change is necessary from Metro-North's main line to an SPV-2000 for the remaining run to Danbury. The view of such sweet towns as Branchville, Redding and Bethel make the trip worthwhile.

*** ***Harlem Line***. Grand Central Station to Dover Plains, New York. Running time two hours, 10 minutes. Once one of the world's best examples of how to turn people away from trains and into autos, the Harlem Line boasts new coaches, tracks and stations and is electrified from Grand Central to Brewster North. From Brewster North to Dover Plains the stock consists of single Budd-type cars going at speeds of 40 mph and under. A remarkable bonus is the lush countryside, especially from Valhalla on north, where the train lumbers past forests and farmlands. Just past Pawling, the train squeezes through a narrow rock cut and continues northward with stops at several stations of considerable quality.

*** ***Hudson Line***. Grand Central Station to Poughkeepsie, New York. Running time, two hours, nine minutes. Objective critics have correctly described this run as one of the most scenic commuter lines in the world. That critique holds, especially if the opening outdoor section from "El Barrio" at Park Avenue and 97th Street to the South Bronx is omitted. From there the train snakes around Spuyten Duyvil, under the Henry Hudson Bridge and turns right for a long, side-by-side tramp with the Hudson River. This is the same vista that once inspired New York Central Railroad press agents to coin the name "Water Level Limited" for, in fact, the Hudson Line hugs water's edge all the way past Peekskill, Croton-Harmon, Beacon and on to Poughkeepsie. Many of the views are spectacular, such as the graceful curve north of Peekskill opening on to panoramic vistas that would make any Rhinelander jealous. Such assets bring out the best in Metro-North employees, who appear to be proud of their Hudson Line. Its rolling stock includes modern electric "Metropolitans" (M-1's and M-3's) from Grand Central to Croton-Harmon and older diesels on to the last stop at Poughkeepsie. With few exceptions, stations fail to sustain the otherwise high qualities of the Hudson line. NOTE: It is important to remember that in order to get the good of the Hudson River views, one must obtain a left side-seat on northbound trains and a right-side seat on southbound runs. Also, morning rides are preferable; the western-setting afternoon sun, reflecting off the river, can become uncomfortable on the shadeless trains.

PATH — HUDSON TUBES

*** ***Newark Line***. World Trade Center to Newark, New Jersey. Running time, 19 minutes. It sounds as if drummer Buddy Rich orchestrated the *paradiddle* rhythms that the click-clack of the Tubes train produces as it sprints across the Jersey meadows and over the Hackensack River. The 1972 rolling stock includes unique Hawker-Siddeley Canada cars built in Thunder Bay, Ontario. PATH is invigorating the system with 95 Kawasaki cars. An added fillip for rail buffs is provided at the Newark terminal, Penn Station. There the rider can walk down a few flights of stairs to the Newark "subway," a trolley car system that plys an interesting route through New Jersey's most maligned metropolis.

** *Jersey City Line*. 33rd Street, Manhattan, to Journal Square, Jersey City, New Jersey. Running time 20 minutes. The original Tubes' 33rd Street terminal was demolished in the 1930's and replaced with newer facilities rubbing shoulders with Gimbel's Basement. The line heads south, stopping at 23rd, 14th, 9th and Christopher streets before dipping down under the Hudson. By the time it reaches Jersey City the train has screeched around some of the sharpest curves in the world. Front-window viewing is a must. (Jersey City is also reached from World Trade Center.)

** *Hoboken Line*. World Trade Center to Hoboken, New Jersey. Running time, nine minutes. When Hudson Terminal (now World Trade Center) opened in July 1909, it was the most elaborate subway station in New York, featuring everything from a meat market to a movie theater. Tubes president William McAdoo boasted a bizarre policy, "The Public Be Pleased," and even offered a system in which a wife could leave purchases made in the city at the Tubes' baggage offices for her husband to pick up later. McAdoo installed a large powder room and supplied the women with free powder and hairpins. He also installed an exclusive restaurant atop the 22-story terminal, anticipating the World Trade Center's Windows On the World restaurant by 68 years. The Hoboken Terminal, reached after stops at Exchange Place and Pavonia Avenue, dates back to February 1908, when fireworks greeted the arrival of the first train from Manhattan. Today, a visitor is best greeted by the Clam Broth House on River Street, just a five-minute stroll from the station. Hoboken, by the way, is the connecting station for many NJ Transit lines. A day trip to Dover with a rest stop at the Clam Broth House is recommended.

STATEN ISLAND RAPID TRANSIT OPERATING AUTHORITY

** *Staten Island Rapid Transit*. St. George (Staten Island Ferry) to Tottenville. Running time, 38 minutes. Step-brother of the BMT (the Staten Island line was supposed to be married to the BMT via a tunnel under the Narrows in the Twenties). Staten Island's contemporary Toonerville rocks and rolls through such aging districts as Tompkinsville, Stapleton and Clifton. Left-hand seats are recommended here for a not-bad view of New York Bay. Once past the Clifton curve, the appeal lessens as the modern rolling stock moves past tract homes, a boarded-up shopping center, Farrell High School and the concrete walls of the open cut between Jefferson Avenue and New Dorp. Once past Princess Bay (one of the prettiest station names anywhere) the vista improves as the train encounters several old homes reeking with character. Tottenville, the last stop, once provided a ferry connection with Perth Amboy, New Jersey. The ferry is long gone but the remnants of the old terminal remain. The gentle waves of Kill van Kull lap against the shore less than ten yards from trainside at the southernmost point in New York State. Tottenville remains a sleepy hamlet within the city limits, sprinkled with Victorian houses and the quietest police precinct (123rd Pct.) in the five boroughs. Unfortunately, the right-of-way and stations of the SIRT are treated with less care and, as a result, the trip from St. George to Tottenville is far less appealing than it could have been if the MTA cared for its own.

World Trade Center, 1971 — Port Authority of NY and NJ

POSTSCRIPT — WHERE DO WE GO FROM HERE?

Depending upon which commuter you poll, service on the suburban lines servicing the New York metropolitan area ranges from delightful to dreadful — with the accent on the latter. Despite the purchase of hundreds of new cars, spread over an assortment of lines; despite promises made by governors, senators, mayors and councilmen; despite blueprints, revised blueprints and the hiring of expensive consultants, commuting by train remains neither the pleasure it should be nor the mode of transportation that it could be.

In some cases beleagured commuters were convinced that service was so bad that it would be impossible to get worse — and then it got worse!

Long Island Rail Road straphangers beefed that trains were late so often that an on-time train was a "shocking experience." Others described train cars as "filthy" and crews as discourteous. "The other day I fell asleep on the train," said one witness, "and a lady ticket-puncher awoke me by kicking me in the leg."

Riders compelled for one reason or another to take the trains have become numbed to a state of bland acceptance of the status quo, no matter how bad. As one LIRR commuter put it, "I would rather get a late train than none at all!"

A Dix Hills, Long Island, rider allowed that continual LIRR delays were "like having a wart on your nose. After a while you get used to it."

For years the consensus among LIRR regulars was that the Oyster Bay branch was the worst of the LIRR's nine lines. A *Newsday* reporter once checked the line out at random and discovered that the ride was bumpy and jerky and in one car the bottom of the toilet was missing, offering a clear view of the tracks below. Another Oyster Bay rider complained that seats were so dirty that she regularly brought a towel to wipe them off. "We are the cleaning crew," she said.

In fairness to the Long Island, it has in the late 1980's shown spurts of improvement, principally because of the attractive rolling stock. But Long Island straphangers have long memories. They recall how, on October 6, 1969, then Governor Nelson Rockefeller stepped to a podium at a breakfast meeting of Long Island business executives to pronounce the LIRR was the finest commuter railroad in the nation. Then, in a fit of braggadoccio, Rockefeller pledged that, "Each day the railroad is going to get finer from now on."

The governor lived to regret that statement and, as *Newsday* duly noted, "Time proved the governor wrong."

Nevertheless, with more and more cars on the road, Long Island motorists may switch to the LIRR as an alternate means of transportation. With precious few highway arteries to and from Manhattan, Long Islanders may be willing to endure limited on-time performance in preference to the tribulations of the Long Island Expressway and Northern State and Southern State parkways.

Riders on the onetime Delaware, Lackawanna and Western Morris and Essex Division have well-appointed and new Arrow rolling stock, which replaced the venerable 1930 Pullman-built coaches on what has been, for some, an always loveable line. In 1971 *Trains* magazine ran a feature about the operation with the caption: "Can commuters love a railroad? Yes."

With completion of the re-electrification of the Morris and Essex, the 18-track stub-end Lackawanna Terminal remains the focal point of the six-county network. As author Fred W.

Schneider, III, noted, the once proud depot ain't what it used to be. "The original polished copper exterior covering has turned green after years of exposure to salt air and pollutants," wrote Schneider. "The 225-foot-high clock tower has vanished. Unchecked, the pigeons ravage the statue of President Samuel Sloan. The Christopher and Barclay Street ferries have passed to oblivion and the muffled voiced of throngs of long-haul passengers are conspicuously absent from the lofty waiting room." With the ferries long gone, most NJ Transit patrons transfer to the PATH Hudson Tubes to complete their journey to Manhattan, although there has been talk of reviving ferry service.

The plan, although not definite, would mean reconstructing the old Hoboken terminal, building a terminal in Manhattan (near the World Trade Center) and purchasing seven new ferries all at a cost of $132 million.

Other alternatives, such as building a new tunnel or increasing capacity on the PATH trains, could take ten to 20 years, cost billions of dollars and cause great inconvenience for regular commuters. The ferries, on the other hand, could be in operation before 1990, and would mean no inconvenience to passengers. However, reservations remain about the ability of the ferry system to meet its operating costs.

While patrons on the Morris and Essex lines are riding their new electrics, other New Jersey Transit commuters have benefited from the acquisition of modern (non-electric) rolling stock, built in the 1970's and 1980's by Pullman-Standard and intelligently designed for ease of conversion to multiple-unit electric cars. Pantograph supports and conduits were installed, while the frame and trucks were designed to accept standard "Jersey Arrow" electrical equipment.

It is generally accepted by railroad critics that the existing Hoboken terminal is obsolete. In 1907, when it was new, the depot was necessary to provide a ferry connection to Manhattan. But it is expensive to heat and maintain and is poorly located, though it provides a link with the Hudson Tubes.

An alternative now under consideration would be to divert all NJ Transit trains onto the tracks leading to Pennsylvania Station. This, however, would not provide new terminal facilities for the Suffern-Port Jervis and Spring Valley trains. Ultimately, these would be linked with the PATH Tubes at Hoboken with a more simplified subway transfer point.

Ironically, as far back as April 1971, *Trains* magazine predicted that the "future does look brighter for the Erie-Lackawanna commuter than it has at any time in the past several decades." Certainly, the outlook in the late 1980's, while not euphoric, should be positive with the improvements on the Morris and Essex lines and the commitment by New Jersey to continue passenger service. As *Trains* so accurately noted, "The true measure of the success of the direction from the capitol will be the continued arrival of the 6:01 at Milburn on time."

Having their trains come in on time is a secondary dream for many commuters in the New York metropolitan area as they look ahead to the late 1980's. Their primary wish is that they simply keep running and — if they are extra lucky — that they obtain a seat for their ride.

There is little cause for excess optimism, an opinion shared by many who study the ebb and flow of the trains.

"Short trains, equipment breakdowns or other delays," commented David A. Andelman in *The New York Times*, "can produce in commuter cars what is known on the subways as 'crush loading.' On the longer commuter runs, however, the 'crush' may have to be endured for trips up to an hour long."

Additionally, the problems of rudeness on the part of railroad personnel, not to mention general insensitivity to the rider, appears to be an area that shows no signs of getting better in the near future — or even distant future, for that matter.

As a regular passenger on the Harlem Division commented when he was informed that there was no heat in the middle of a bitterly cold January morning, "That problem will be solved by body heat any minute now."

The passenger, naturally, was right. His coach soon filled to capacity, with barely enough room to breathe. At the next station a loudspeaker announcement proclaimed, "Seats in the rear, seats in the rear."

The inducement was not at all persuasive to the veteran commuters. "Nobody believes it," a passenger charged. "Why? Because of years of lying. The other lie is 'Train right behind with lots of seats.' That's worse. There's no train behind and there are no seats."

Hardened by their tribulations, many straphangers are quite willing to put up with standing-room-only conditions as long as the trains get them where they want to go, and within minutes of the scheduled arrival time. "But," explained one veteran, "with trains so crowded, the schedules get delayed. And one delay here or there and the entire line backs up."

When all is said and done the sorry plight of the commuter railroads will remain well into the 1990's unless both the federal and state governments commit themselves to spending the huge sums necessary to develop and maintain these vital transportation facilties.

Until then, passengers on the nation's largest commuter rail network can expect to be bothered and bewildered by their predicament.

Some of them may even buy another car.

THE END